what really counts
for men

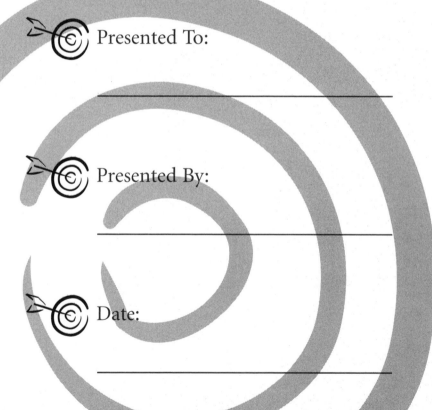

Presented To:

_____

Presented By:

_____

Date:

_____

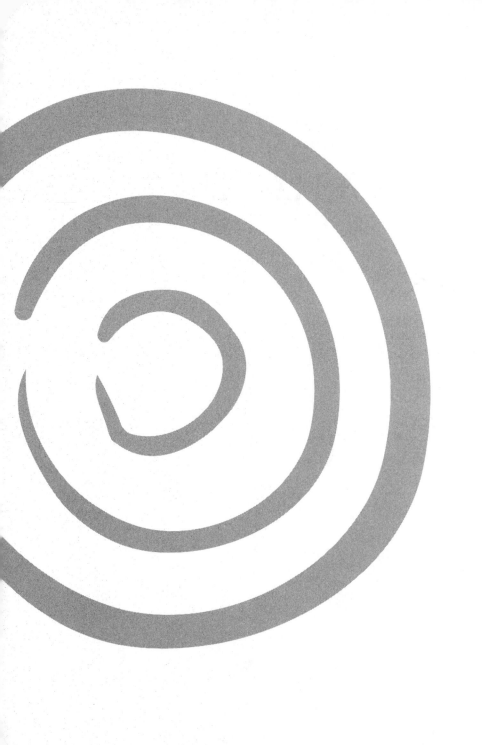

what
really
counts
for men

NELSON BOOKS
A Division of Thomas Nelson Publishers
Since 1798

www.thomasnelson.com

Published in Nashville, Tennessee, by Thomas Nelson, Inc.

Managing Editor: Lila Empson
Editor: Kyle Olund
Manuscript: J. Heyward Rogers
Design: Thatcher Design, Nashville, TN

Library of Congress Cataloging-in-Publication Data

What really counts for men.
    p. cm.
  ISBN 0-7852-0950-6 (pbk.)
  1. Christian men—Religious life. I. Thomas Nelson Publishers.
BV4528.2.W45 2005
248.8'42—dc22

2005024964

Printed in the United States of America

05 06 07 08 09 QWK 5 4 3 2 1

Live out this God-created identity
the way our Father lives toward us,
generously and graciously, even
when we're at our worst.

LUKE 6:35 MSG

Contents

Introduction

**Walk in Him, rooted and built up
in Him and established in the faith, as
you have been taught, abounding in it
with thanksgiving.**

COLOSSIANS 2:6–7 NKJV

Demands for your time and attention are constantly coming at you from all directions—from your career, your family, your friends, your church. Then there are your own internal desires for fulfillment and significance. You feel the unmistakable urge to leave a mark on the world you live in. That's what it means to be a grown man with responsibilities.

Life is a series of choices. If you're going to make good choices—choices that will lead you on to do better things and to make a positive difference in the lives of the people around you—you need to know what really counts. That's what this book is about.

What Really Counts for Men features motivating stories, thought-provoking quotations, and stimulating Scripture verses. It is a guide that distills biblical wisdom about what God says really counts in your reality and life experience. You'll find new insights to steer you in your decisions and to give you ideas about what is important and what isn't.

In some ways, choosing between good and bad isn't that hard. The hard thing is choosing between good and better, between better and best. Those choices become a whole lot easier if you've already decided what really counts.

—J. Heyward Rogers

LIFE

An Introduction

> I have come that they may have life, and that they may have it more abundantly.
>
> JOHN 10:10 NKJV

The apostle Paul speaks of Christians as being "in the world but not of the world." It's a delicate balancing act: Your true home is heaven, and yet, here you are. You aren't whisked away to heaven the moment you receive Christ. How, then, do you make this time on earth count? More to the point, how do you make your time on earth count without counting too much on the things of earth?

what really counts

You know you're supposed to keep an eternal perspective, but you still have to make a living like everybody else. You still have to deal with difficult people, some of whom live in your very house. Your car still breaks down. You have deadlines and mortgage payments. On the one hand it all seems so mundane. You know there's more to life than this. Nevertheless, it all seems so much more real than an eternal hereafter that you can't see or smell or hear. How are you supposed to keep an eternal perspective when you have bunions and the boss is on your case?

It's helpful to remember that eternity is now. It's not something that starts after you die. Your eternal life is already in full swing. What's more, the vast sweep of eternity doesn't render this life insignificant. Rather, as you live in light of heaven, life on earth is more and more significant. For once you realize that this life isn't all there is, you can begin to live this life to its fullest.

> This life was not intended to be the place of our perfection, but the preparatory for it.
>
> RICHARD BAXTER

Life
The Big Picture

> Man is like a breath; his days are
> like a passing shadow.
> PSALM 144:4 NKJV

How long do you plan to live? Seventy years? Eighty years? A hundred? Try an eternity. You are going to live forever. Even if your earthly life turned out to be a thousand years long, it would still be the merest blink compared to the eternal life that stretches out before you. Life on earth is just a first step, a baby step, in your eternal life. That kind of perspective should change the way you think about the world.

David prayed for the wisdom to see how short earthly life really is: "LORD, remind me how brief my time on earth will be. Remind me that my days are numbered, and that my life is fleeing away. My life is no longer than the width of my hand. An entire lifetime is just a moment to you; human existence is but a breath" (Psalm 39:4–5 NLT).

Seems like a strange prayer, doesn't it? Why pray to be reminded that death is coming? Because the better you understand life's shortness, the less likely you are to let mere earthly pursuits get in the way of the business of heaven.

You probably work forty or so hours every week. Do you ever give any thought to how you might use those hours to have an eternal impact on the people in your sphere of influence? Remember, they're going to live forever too. You may be a father. Does your relationship with your kids help them understand what it means to be the child of a heavenly father? It's all about your mindset. As Colossians 3:2 puts it, "Set your minds on what is above" (HCSB). That doesn't mean you should become a monk or quit your job or sell all your belongings. You still have an earthly life to live. The question is whether or not you invest that earthly life to gain eternal wealth.

Sure, the world you see when you look around appears to be real and solid. It is, but it's also temporary. If this is all there is, what's the point of all the effort you put forth? "We make our pile, and then we leave it" (Psalm 39:6 MSG). Any riches, any accomplishments you accumulate on earth are going to go away, but the treasure that you pile up in the eternal economy is treasure that will last forever. That's the only kind of treasure that lasts as long as you will.

Life
The Big Picture

What Matters Most...

◉ Seeking God first. This is the key to abundant life; this is how you have it all.

◉ Tending to your soul. That's the real you—your eternal self.

◉ Loving other people. Long after the things of earth are gone, they will live on.

◉ Building the kingdom of God. No earthly kingdom compares.

◉ Living eternal life. There's more to life than life on earth.

What **Doesn't** Matter...

◉ Your pile of stuff. The person who dies with the most toys dies anyway.

◉ Your earthly status. Your real status is defined in heaven.

◉ Your long-term plans. Only God knows the number of your days.

◉ Being first. In the end, the first will be last.

◉ Anything whose significance dies when your body dies.

Focus Points...

Teach us how short our lives really are so that we may be wise.
PSALM 90:12 NCV

If anyone builds on this foundation with gold, silver, precious stones, wood, hay, straw, each one's work will become clear; for the Day will declare it, because it will be revealed by fire; and the fire will test each one's work, of what sort it is.
1 CORINTHIANS 3:12–13 NKJV

Don't store treasures for yourselves here on earth where moths and rust will destroy them and thieves can break in and steal them. But store your treasures in heaven where they cannot be destroyed by moths or rust and where thieves cannot break in and steal them.
MATTHEW 6:19–20 NCV

what really counts

Set your mind on things above, not on things on the earth.
COLOSSIANS 3:2 NKJV

We take excellent care of our bodies which we have for only a lifetime; yet we let our souls shrivel which we will have for eternity.

BILLY GRAHAM

The greatest use of life is to spend it for something that will outlast it.

WILLIAM JAMES

Life
One Life to Live

There is a time for everything, and everything on earth has its special season.

ECCLESIASTES 3:1 NCV

what really counts

The Romans said *carpe diem*—seize the day. Make hay while the sun shines, or, as a recent ad campaign puts it, grab life by the horns. The apostle Paul had his own version of those slogans: "Be careful how you walk, not as unwise men but as wise, making the most of your time, because the days are evil" (Ephesians 5:15–16 NASB).

Life is short, and there's so much to do—at home, at work, at church, on the ball field, in volunteer organizations. Life sometimes feels like one long series of emergencies. Just when you get one fire put out, another one flares up. Now you have the apostle Paul piling more guilt on you: Make the most of your days. Has he seen your schedule lately? There's one thing you should understand about that exhortation. It's not a call to more busyness. It's not a command to crank up the pace in an already hectic life. That's not the way of peace that Jesus offers. Can you even imagine Jesus in a hurry? Can you imagine Him being too busy to talk to a child or help a person in need or speak the truth to somebody who needs to hear it?

Paul's command to "make the most of your time" is a call to do the right things, not more things. It's a call to put first things first so that the urgent things in your life don't elbow out the important things. It's easy to lose sight of the difference. Something is always screaming for your attention, but God often whispers. It takes discipline to stay focused on what really matters. It doesn't, however, take a genius. People matter more than things. Love matters more than self-indulgence. The things of heaven matter more than the things of earth.

In the book of Ephesians, Paul speaks of good works that God has "prepared beforehand that we should walk in them" (Ephesians 2:10 NKJV). You have work to do in this life. You have time to do it; God hasn't laid out for you more work than will fit in your allotted time. Nevertheless, the time you lose—whether in sloth and laziness or in irrelevant busyness—is lost forever. Make the most of the days you have. Your time is too valuable to waste on the merely urgent.

Life
One Life to Live

What Matters Most...

- Making the most of your time. Every day is a gift from God.

- Setting your priorities. Make sure your daily routine reflects what matters most from a heavenly perspective.

- Cultivating relationships. If you're too busy to reach out to others, you're too busy.

- Worshiping God. Eternity is now. By connecting you to the eternal, worship gives meaning to your earthly life.

- Being quiet. As you plan your day, build in time to reflect.

What ▮▮▮▮▮ Matter...

- Urgency. Something is always screaming for your attention. Ask "How important is this?" not "How urgent is this?"

- Busyness. A full schedule isn't the same thing as a full life.

- Ambition. Your worth is in Christ, not in earthly achievements. Focus on your place in God's kingdom, and you'll find your place in the world.

- Empty amusements. You can't kill time without injuring eternity.

- Procrastination. Your time belongs to God.

Focus Points...

God chose you to be his people, so I urge you now to live the life to which God called you.
EPHESIANS 4:1 NCV

Be diligent to present yourself approved to God, a worker who does not need to be ashamed, rightly dividing the word of truth.
2 TIMOTHY 2:15 NKJV

The plans of the diligent lead surely to plenty, but those of everyone who is hasty, surely to poverty.
PROVERBS 21:5 NKJV

There is one thing I always do. Forgetting the past and straining toward what is ahead, I keep trying to reach the goal and get the prize for which God called me through Christ to the life above.
PHILIPPIANS 3:13–14 NCV

what really counts

Wherever you are, be all there. Live to the hilt every situation you believe to be the will of God.

JIM ELLIOT

Life is not just a few years to spend on self-indulgence and career advancement. It is a privilege, a responsibility, a stewardship to be lived according to a much higher calling, God's calling. This alone gives true meaning to life.

ELIZABETH DOLE

21

What Matters Most to Me About
Life

A Christian is called to set his mind on the things of heaven rather than on the things of earth. He is also called to make the most of the short time he has here. It's a balancing act. The following questions may help you start thinking about how to achieve that balance.

◎ *Your eternal life is well underway; eternity doesn't start after you die. How does that realization change the way you think about life on earth?*

_____

_____

_____

_____

_____

_____

_____

◎ *What really matters to you about life? Make a list. Now consider how you spend your time. How closely do the two lists correlate?*

_____

_____

_____

_____

_____

_____

_____

_____

◉ *If you knew you had only one week left on earth, what would you do differently?*

_____

_____

_____

_____

_____

_____

_____

_____

_____

◉ *How are you investing your earthly life—time, money, resources— in order to gain eternal wealth?*

_____

_____

_____

_____

_____

_____

_____

_____

_____

_____

Life's a voyage that's homeward bound.
HERMAN MELVILLE

GOD

An Introduction

> Our God is in heaven; He does whatever He pleases.
>
> PSALM115:3 NKJV

what really counts

The philosopher Blaise Pascal observed that the single most distinguishing feature of God's all-encompassing power is the fact that "our imagination gets lost when thinking about it." The same thing is true of any of God's attributes. God is everywhere at the same time. Try getting your mind around that. He exists beyond time. Our time-bound imaginations can't begin to grasp such a thing. He knows and understands everything. It makes your head hurt even to imagine it. Because God is infinite, there are things about Him that finite human beings can never know." 'My thoughts are not your thoughts, nor are your ways My ways,' says the LORD" (Isaiah 55:8 NKJV).

However, if God's infinity is mind-boggling, there is

another aspect of His personality that is just as hard to fathom. That's the fact that He loves us and sees fit to make Himself known to us. "The secret things belong to the LORD our God, but those things which are revealed belong to us and to our children forever" (Deuteronomy 29:29 NKJV).

The knowledge of God—as far as human beings can know Him—is your inheritance. Revel in it. Bask in it. For as you dwell on the truths of God, your faith in Him will grow, and you will enjoy Him more and more. Yes there are mysteries. But you can rest even in the mysteries, content in the knowledge that one day you will be with God, and you will be like Him, for you will see Him as He is (1 John 3:2).

One with God is a majority.

BILLY GRAHAM

God
The Beginning and the End

The sky was made at the Lord's command. By the breath from his mouth, he made all the stars.
PSALM 33:6 NCV

"Where did I come from?" It's probably the most fundamental of all religious questions. It might sound at first like a question with a scientific answer. A quick review of biological facts seems to offer some enlightenment, but all that really does is to push the original question back toward its source: "Yes, but where did the biological facts come from?" There are theories for where the biological facts came from too, but in the end, all theories, all hypotheses run up against one very simple fact: Something cannot come from nothing. The universe is an awe-inspiring place—in its beauty, its intricacy, its size; in its power, its delicacy, its detail, but as amazing as it is, there's one thing your soul tells you about this universe: It didn't make itself.

Perhaps that's why the first sentence of Scripture addresses the question of origins: "In the beginning, God created the heavens and the earth." The oldest creeds of the Christian faith start at the same place: "I believe in God, the Father almighty, maker of heaven and earth." The most basic relationship between God and you is that of Creator and creature. The entire universe is God's handiwork, you included.

God's claim on you, however, is not merely that of creator to creation, or of owner to possession. His claim on you is a claim of love. God made you to fellowship with Him. He made you to partake of Him, to be like Him. That's why He made you in His own image, so that you could be something that the rest of the creation—animals and rocks and trees—could never be. The Genesis creation account describes God speaking the world into existence, but when it came time to make human beings, God took the dust of the earth and lovingly shaped it into a human form. Then He breathed His own breath into Adam's body to give it life.

The breath of the Creator is your very life. It's an astonishing thing to think about. Your life-source isn't of this world. For all its wonders, the world that you see, hear, touch, smell, and taste isn't what gave you being. God made you. He made you in His image. Every breath you take follows from that first, supernatural breath, when God breathed His own life to Adam.

God
The Beginning and the End

What Matters Most...

◎ The majesty of God in His creation. Heaven and earth show forth God's glory and tell what kind of God made you.

◎ Where you came from. God made you to fellowship with Him.

◎ God's claim on you. He is the Potter, you are the clay. His claim on you is more one of love than one of ownership.

◎ God's image in you. If you are in Christ, that likeness is being restored as you are conformed to the image of Christ.

◎ God's breath in you. You aren't as ordinary as you may think.

What **Doesn't** Matter...

◎ The things you cannot understand. God surpasses your comprehension, but He has revealed more than enough of Himself to keep your head and heart and imagination busy.

◎ Your finitude. God invites you to partake of infinity with Him.

◎ Your feelings of insignificance. You are God's unique creation.

◎ Skeptics. In His creation, God has given ample evidence of His existence.

Focus Points...

By faith, we see the world called into existence by God's word, what we see created by what we don't see.
HEBREWS 11:3 MSG

There are things about him that people cannot see—his eternal power and all the things that make him God. But since the beginning of the world those things have been easy to understand by what God has made.
ROMANS 1:20 NCV

The heavens declare the glory of God; and the firmament shows His handiwork. Day unto day utters speech, and night unto night reveals knowledge.
PSALM 19:1–2 NKJV

You are worthy, O Lord our God, to receive glory and honor and power. For you created everything, and it is for your pleasure that they exist and were created.
REVELATION 4:11 NLT

what really counts

God is seen in the star, in the stone, in the flesh, in the soul and the clod.

ROBERT BROWNING

The deepest desire of our hearts is for union with God. God created us for union with himself. This is the original purpose of our lives.

BRENNAN MANNING

God
God Is Love

The person who refuses to love doesn't know
the first thing about God, because God is love—
so you can't know him if you don't love.

1 JOHN 4:8 MSG

what really counts

In the movie *Raising Arizona*, H. I. and Ed McDonough,
an ex-convict and his police-officer wife, enjoy a happy life
together in their little love-nest of a mobile home in the
Arizona desert. There's only one thing missing: They yearn
for a baby to share their life with. Ed feels the longing most
acutely. As H. I. puts it, "her point was that there was too
much love and beauty for just the two of us." It's a beautiful
thing to think about—a love so nearly perfect that the only
way to improve on it is to have another person to be the
object of their love.

If the first religious question is "Where did I come from?"
the second question must be "Why am I here?" You are here
because God felt something similar to what Ed McDonough
felt. Though already perfect, the three-personed God desired
to have people on whom to lavish so much love and beauty.
You are here to be the object of God's perfect love.

God is love, and it is by loving that He expresses who He is. Or to put it another way, it is by loving that God shines forth His glory. God doesn't love His people because they have earned His love, or because they have lived up to His expectations. He doesn't love them because He needs them on His team. Consider God's word to the Israelites: "The LORD did not set his love on you nor choose you because you were more in number than any other people, for you were the least of all peoples; but because the LORD loves you" (Deuteronomy 7:7–8 NKJV). It's a peculiar and striking bit of reasoning: God loves you because He loves you. Human beings sometimes have ulterior motives for loving one another, but not God. You aren't a means toward some other end. Except one, maybe: God loves you in order to show the universe what kind of God He is. God needs no other reason to love. He's just being Himself.

"This is love, not that we loved God, but that He loved us" (1 John 4:10 NKJV). That's a love you can rest in. It doesn't depend on your ability to be lovable or to deserve love; rather, it depends on the unfailing character of the God who *is* love. That's a love that casts out all fear.

God
God Is Love

What Matters Most...

◎ God's love for you. It's lavish. It's extravagant. By loving you He shines forth His glory.

◎ Your love for God. You love in response to the God who loved you first.

◎ Your love for others. Genuine love is a direct result of God's love overflowing from you.

◎ God's character. The certainty of God's love is based on the perfection of His faithfulness.

◎ Your rest. Relax. Nothing can separate you from the love of God.

What **Doesn't** Matter...

◎ Your past. God's love is new every morning.

◎ Your doubts. They don't affect God's love for you.

◎ Your fear. Perfect love cases out fear.

◎ Your character flaws. God loves you because of His character, not because of your character.

◎ Your failures. You aren't earning God's love anyway. He loves you no matter what.

Focus Points...

As the Father loved Me, I also have loved you; abide in My love.
JOHN 15:9 NKJV

God's mercy is great, and he loved us very much. Though we were spiritually dead because of the things we did against God, he gave us new life with Christ. You have been saved by God's grace.
EPHESIANS 2:4–5 NCV

This is how much God loved the world: He gave His Son, His one and only Son. And this is why: so that no one need be destroyed; by believing in him, anyone can have a whole and lasting life.
JOHN 3:16 MSG

what really counts

I am persuaded that neither death nor life, nor angels nor principalities nor powers, nor things present nor things to come, nor height nor depth, nor any other created thing, shall be able to separate us from the love of God which is in Christ Jesus our Lord.
ROMANS 8:38–39 NKJV

God loves you right where you are, but he doesn't want to leave you there.

MAX LUCADO

God's gifts put man's best dreams to shame.

ELIZABETH BARRETT BROWNING

33

God

God Is in Control

Two sparrows cost only a penny, but not even one of them can die without your Father's knowing it. God even knows how many hairs are on your head. So don't be afraid. You are worth much more than many sparrows.

MATTHEW 10:29–31 NCV

what really counts

Have you ever seen an impressionist painting up close? If you stand a foot away from the canvas, all you see is blobs of color, lumpy and seemingly random. A splat of yellow spills over onto a splotch of purple next to a smear of brown. But as you take a step back and take in the whole picture, it becomes apparent that a very skilled artist had a plan all along. The splats and blobs arrange themselves into a picture of depth and richness and vibrancy.

When you look at the world around you, things can seem pretty random. You see good and decent people suffering while the wicked prosper. You see friends and loved ones get sick and die. You lose your job because of a random decision in a corporate headquarters a thousand miles away. You read the news. War. Terrorism. Violent crime. Broken families. Is God in control or not?

God is in control. He knows how many hairs are on your head. Not even a sparrow falls to the ground outside of God's will. Every event, every moment, every atom of the universe is under the direction of the God, who is not only the Creator but the Sustainer too. That may seem like cold comfort at first. What good is it for God to be in control if he's still going to let bad things happen to good people? Nevertheless, in the end it's the only comfort there is. The God who has the whole universe in His hands makes "all things work together for good to those who love God, to those who are the called according to His purpose" (Romans 8:28 NKJV). As R. C. Sproul has pointed out, if there is so much as one molecule out there that is not under God's control, then God is not God. For that one maverick molecule could be the grain of sand that gets into the machinery of God's providence and throws His whole purpose out of whack.

Living here on earth is a little bit like looking at an impressionist painting from a foot away. Things can look splotchy, lumpy, and random, but one day you will see the whole image, and it will become apparent that the divine Artist of the universe was ordering all those little blobs of light and darkness and color into a picture of depth and beauty and abundance.

God
God Is in Control

What Matters Most...

◎ God's perfect plan. All things fit together into a beautiful whole.

◎ God's perfect love. He wants what's best for you.

◎ God's omniscience. He knows what's best for you, and no detail has escaped His notice.

◎ God's omnipotence. Nothing can keep Him from carrying out His plan.

◎ God's omnipresence. He's always with you, no matter what you're going through.

What Doesn't Matter...

◎ Human shortsightedness. You can't take in the whole big picture; not yet, anyway.

◎ Randomness. It's only an illusion. God is always in control.

◎ Plan B. God's plan is the only plan, however human beings think they can improve on it.

◎ Impatience. Someday you will be able to look back at the beauty of God's plan. But that may not be today.

◎ Human power, when it sets itself against the purposes of God, that is. God does as He pleases.

Focus Points...

Everything comes from him; everything happens through him; everything ends up in him. Always glory! Always praise! Yes. Yes. Yes.
ROMANS 11:36 MSG

Life on this earth doesn't add up to much, but God's heavenly army keeps everything going. No one can interrupt his work, no one can call his rule into question.
DANIEL 4:35 MSG

The nations raged, the kingdoms were moved; He uttered His voice, the earth melted. The LORD of hosts is with us; the God of Jacob is our refuge . . . Be still, and know that I am God; I will be exalted among the nations, I will be exalted in the earth!
PSALM 46:6–7, 10 NKJV

what really counts

I know that you can do all things, and that no purpose of yours can be thwarted.
JOB 42:2 NRSV

If God has made your cup sweet, drink it with grace. If he has made it bitter, drink it in communion with him.
OSWALD CHAMBERS

Never be afraid to trust an unknown future to a known God.
CORRIE TEN BOOM

God
The Apple of God's Eye

> Keep me as the apple of Your eye; hide me under the shadow of Your wings.
>
> PSALM 17:8 NKJV

what really counts

What do you think God thinks about you? Many people imagine God as being permanently mad and frustrated at them, perhaps because they are so often frustrated with themselves for staying in the same ruts and falling into the same bad habits. It can be hard to believe what the Bible says about God's love and forgiveness. Or perhaps you believe it in your head but you don't feel the effects of that truth down in your heart. Maybe you imagine God offers a grudging pardon, a reluctant love. Maybe you picture God as barely tolerating you, the way a boss puts up with a bad employee he cannot fire.

Consider what the prophet Zephaniah said about the way God feels about His people: "he will rejoice over you with gladness, he will renew you in his love; he will exult over you with loud singing" (Zephaniah 3:17 NRSV). It's hard to fathom, isn't it? The God of Heaven rejoices over you. Isaiah says the same thing in a different way: "as the bridegroom rejoices over the bride, so shall your God rejoice over you" (Isaiah 62:5 NKJV). There's nothing reluctant or reserved about that kind of joy.

It's one of the great mysteries, how God can hate sin without staying perpetually angry and upset, when you consider all the sinners running loose in the world He created. Yet, as John Piper asks, "What if God were frustrated and despondent and gloomy and dismal and dejected?" Piper answers his own question: "We would all relate to God like little children who have a frustrated, gloomy, dismal, discontented father. They can't enjoy him. They can only try not to bother him, and maybe try to work for him to earn some little favor." That's not the kind of God you serve. He's a joyous God, and if you are in Christ, He joys in you. You are released from the nagging belief that God wishes He had never agreed to love and forgive you. God loves to love you.

Because of Christ's satisfactory work, God is fully satisfied with you. That doesn't mean you're perfect. God will still smooth off your rough edges and finish out the work He has begun in you. In the meantime, He rejoices over you the way a father rejoices over his son. You are the apple of His eye.

God
The Apple of God's Eye

What Matters Most...

◎ Believing that God rejoices in you. You are the apple of His eye.

◎ Feeling God's joy in you. God's joy is a source of strength and hope.

◎ Reflecting God's joy back to Him. God's joy becomes your joy.

◎ Turning to God every day. His mercies are new every morning.

◎ Prospering under God's blessing. This is how true abundance starts to take hold in your life.

What **Doesn't** Matter...

◎ The times you don't feel God's joy. Return to Him. Press on.

◎ The condemning voice of Satan. If God is for you, who can be against you?

◎ The barriers you put between yourself and God's joy. You can't hide from God.

◎ The seeming impossibility (when you've blown it) that God could possibly rejoice in someone like you.

◎ The sneaking suspicion (when you're doing well) that you deserve such lavish love from God.

Focus Points...

May the glory of the LORD be forever. May the LORD enjoy what he has made.
PSALM 104:31 NCV

The LORD takes pleasure in his people; he honors the humble with victory. Let God's people rejoice in their triumph and sing joyfully all night long.
PSALM 149:4–5 GNT

Let them shout for joy and be glad, who favor my righteous cause; and let them say continually, "Let the LORD be magnified, who has pleasure in the prosperity of His servant."
PSALM 35:27 NKJV

Yes, I [God] will rejoice over them to do them good, and I will assuredly plant them in this land, with all My heart and with all My soul.
JEREMIAH 32:41 NKJV

what really counts

Let your faith in Christ be in the quiet confidence that He will every day and moment keep you as the apple of His eye, keep you in perfect peace and in the sure experience of all the light and the strength you need.

ANDREW MURRAY

Can't you see the Creator of the universe, who understands every secret, every mystery ... sitting patiently and listening to a four-year-old talk to Him? That's a beautiful image of a father.

JAMES DOBSON

What Matters Most to Me About
God

The secret things belong to God. A finite human mind has no hope of comprehending the infinity of God, but where God has revealed Himself, it is the privilege and duty of believers to contemplate those things.

◉ *Skies, seas, mountains, swamps, forests, tundra—all God's works declare His glory. "Unspoken truth is spoken everywhere" (Psalm 19:4 MSG). When was the last time the natural world taught you something about the nature of God?*

_____

_____

_____

_____

_____

_____

_____

_____

◉ *"God is love." How is that different from saying "Love is God"?*

_____

_____

_____

_____

_____

_____

_____

Though life is lived forward, it is often only understood looking backward. Write about a time when you have seen God's hand at work for your good in circumstances that at the time seemed to be negative or random.

_____

_____

_____

_____

_____

_____

_____

_____

_____

Do you find it hard to believe that the God of the universe rejoices over you with loud singing? Why or why not?

_____

_____

_____

_____

_____

_____

_____

_____

_____

_____

True religion is a union of God with the soul, a real participation of the divine nature, the very image of God drawn upon the soul.

HENRY SCOUGAL

JESUS

An Introduction

> We have fixed our hope on the living God, who is the Savior of all men, especially of believers.
>
> 1 TIMOTHY 4:10 NASB

what really counts

It is a well-known fact that Jesus Christ was a great man who revolutionized the world. No serious historian would dispute that. Most calendars set the date as the number of years since His birth. Roman, Greek, and Jewish scholars are all in agreement that He existed, but the case for Christianity rests on a single claim of His. Jesus said, "If you had known Me, you would have known My Father also; and from now on you know Him and have seen Him" (John 14:7 NKJV).

Jesus claimed that He was God. He wasn't just a good person. You can choose to reject what He said and call Him a liar, or you can think He was a little deluded and call Him crazy. The alternative, of course, is to accept His claims and honor Him as Lord. Songwriter Toby McKeehan said, "In a world that consists of fake lives and false promises, Jesus is authentic, and He died on the cross to prove it."

Most people in the world agree that there is some kind of divine being out there who is in charge of life. That kind of god, who is nameless and formless, is easy to talk about. That kind of god might fill you with the warm fuzzies, but he won't be there to save you. However, when you accept the words of Jesus as truth, you have a whole standard by which to live. His words can cut through your soul and make you a new man.

You should point to the whole man Jesus and say, "That is God."

MARTIN LUTHER

Jesus
God Made Flesh

The Word became flesh and made his dwelling among us. We have seen his glory, the glory of the One and Only ... full of grace and truth.

JOHN 1:14 NIV

In the Old Testament, God revealed Himself as fire from a bush, smoke from a mountain, and the voice of thunder. Those privileged enough to meet His angelic messengers face to face were full of fear in their brilliant presence, but he never became a human being and walked among human beings as one of them. At the ordained time, God chose to take on a human body and voice. When He did, He fulfilled more than 300 prophecies that described the details of His life. His name became Jesus, the Christ.

The great church father Athanasius said that when God took on human form, He never lost His deity; He only added His humanity. The prophet Samuel wrote, "As for God, His way is perfect" (2 Samuel 22:31 NKJV). He remained perfect as God in the flesh, describing Himself as "the way" (John 14:6). When He spoke as an earthly teacher, He used examples that people would understand: seeds thrown along a path, fruit

46

growing on a vine, treasures of golden coins. He told stories of His kingdom and healed painful diseases.

As He walked the earth, Jesus often touched His creation. When He was hungry, He picked wheat off the stalks with His disciples. When thousands were hungry, He fed them with loaves of bread and fish. With His own hands, He broke the loaves of bread. He held children on His lap and blessed them. He mixed spit with mud to give sight to a blind man who had never seen. As God the Creator, He designed all living things; as Jesus of Nazareth, God the Son, He was able to experience them fully.

God chose to identify with you, so that you can identify with Him. Because He humbled Himself to become a man like you, He has the capacity to understand your joys and sorrows. When you go to Him in suffering, He knows your pain because He also wept and bled. When you offer your voice in songs of praise, He knows the joy of singing with a human voice. As Jesus, God ate and drank and laughed and slept and dreamed. Before He died, He said, "If I am lifted up from the earth, I will draw all people toward me" (John 12:32 NCV). Because God became flesh and entered into your world, He has opened the door for you to enter His.

Jesus
God Made Flesh

What Matters Most...

◉ His love. He loves you so much He died a human death to save you.

◉ His joy. He takes pleasure in all His creation, especially His people.

◉ His passion. He experienced the depth of all our emotions.

◉ His pain. He felt rejected, He wept, He bled.

◉ His glory. He is the image of almighty God in the flesh.

What Doesn't Matter...

◉ Who you were before you met Him. Who you were is forgotten and in your past.

◉ What He looked like. You'll find out someday.

◉ When exactly He will come again. Your only choice is to be ready.

◉ Why He chose to do it the way He did. His plan existed from the beginning.

◉ How God became a man. You'll learn the details in heaven.

Focus Points...

If you really knew me, you would know my Father as well. From now on, you do know him and have seen him.
JOHN 14:7 NIV

The Son reflects the glory of God and shows exactly what God is like.
HEBREWS 1:3 NCV

He was in the beginning with God. All things were made through Him, and without Him nothing was made that was made.
JOHN 1:2–3 NKJV

He is the image of the invisible God, the firstborn of all creation.
COLOSSIANS 1:15 NASB

what really counts

The doctrine of Jesus' two natures is important, because if it isn't true, we can't be saved. If he's not God, then he can't reach to God for us, and if he's not man, he can't reach to man.

NORMAN GEISLER

.

"Just call me Jesus," you can almost hear him say. He was the kind of fellow you'd invite to watch the Rams-Giants game at your house ... He'd laugh at your jokes and tell a few of his own. And when you spoke, he'd listen to you as if he had all the time in eternity.

MAX LUCADO

Jesus
The Perfect Example

> As the Spirit of the Lord works within us, we become more and more like him and reflect his glory even more.
>
> 2 CORINTHIANS 3:18 NLT

Perfection. You aim for it every day, whether intentionally or not. You'd like to be that perfect man who says the right words, makes the right financial decisions, and pleases everyone. Then at the end of the day, you could kick back and enjoy the fruit of your efforts. You'd have no struggles overcoming temptation, no angry words searing your conscience, and no worries about your future. You'd be the walking epitome of excellence.

But reality's not like that. A gap always exists between you and perfection, no matter how hard you try. The only perfect human to walk the earth was Jesus, and He lived the perfect, sinless life because He was fully God in the flesh. History pivots on the point when God entered the world as a baby born of woman. At His birth, angels sang His glory and shepherds traveled to worship him. He helped His earthly father in carpentry and obeyed His parents. Scripture says He "grew in wisdom and stature, and in favor with God and men" (Luke 2:52 NIV). He never once sinned.

When He began His ministry at age thirty, He touched those who were dirty, loved those whom everyone else rejected, and forgave those who hated Him. He wisely resisted the temptations of the evil one. His compassion for people energized Him, even when He was grieving and weary. The majority of His time was spent in training His disciples, who would continue long after Him. He washed their feet in order to teach them to be servants and said, "I did this as an example so that you should do as I have done for you" (John 13:15 NCV).

Jesus is the perfect example. He showed humanity the way living should be done. You'd like to live that way, but it's an impossible task on your own strength. Most men of strong, godly character will be the first to admit that they're nothing without Christ. When you allow Jesus to live and breathe His words through you, the impossible can become possible through His strength. Begin your day on your knees, seeking His help. Read the four Gospels repeatedly, focusing on the words, sometimes printed in red, of the mighty God who humbled His deity to become flesh. Allow Him to conform you more to His image, for one day you will meet Him in perfection, face to face.

Jesus
The Perfect Example

What Matters Most...

◎ Following the perfect example of Christ through daily obedience.

◎ Focusing on renewing your mind through Scripture. Scripture allows you to meet Jesus.

◎ Forgiving others and moving on, as Christ did. No good comes from dwelling on the wrong.

◎ Fleeing temptations. Practice resisting the evil one, just as Jesus did.

◎ Fellowshipping with other believers. By doing so you can add your strength to theirs.

What **Doesn't** Matter...

◎ Your worries. He'll provide.

◎ Your impatience. He'll work in His time. God's timetable is based on many factors you may be unaware of.

◎ Your regrets. He'll cleanse you. Jesus had a deep compassion for you.

◎ Your lack of faith. He'll meet you. A good way to begin the morning is on your knees.

◎ Your mistakes. He'll forgive you. Jesus touched those whom others rejected.

Focus Points...

For our sake he made him to be sin who knew no sin, so that in him we might become the righteousness of God.
2 Corinthians 5:21 NRSV

Your attitude should be the same as that of Christ Jesus: Who, being in very nature God . . . made himself nothing, taking the very nature of a servant.
Philippians 2:5–7 NIV

God knew them before he made the world, and he decided that they would be like his Son so that Jesus would be the firstborn of many brothers.
Romans 8:29 NCV

This is to continue until all of us are united in our faith and in our knowledge about God's Son, until we become mature, until we measure up to Christ, who is the standard.
Ephesians 4:13 GOD'S WORD

Being obedient to Christ is a twenty-four-hour-a-day thing. We don't put him on and take him off like a suit of clothes. We have to live God.

Charles Colson

Christlikeness is not produced by imitation, but by inhabitation. We allow Christ to live through us.

Rick Warren

53

Jesus
The Perfect Sacrifice

> Christ was offered as a sacrifice one time to take away the sins of many people. And he will come a second time, not to offer Himself for sin, but to bring salvation to those who are waiting for him.
>
> HEBREWS 9:28 NCV

what really counts

A fireman clad in heavy rescue gear and boots runs upstairs into a burning building to save lives. A brave soldier charges into the line of machine-gun fire on a dusty battle-field. A rescuer dives into icy waters to retrieve a lost swim-mer. What do all these heroes have in common? They don't think twice about sacrificing their lives for the good of others. If you asked them why, they'd probably say, "I'm just doing my job. I'm following the orders of the one in charge."

In the same way, when Jesus submitted Himself to death on the cross, He said, "Here I am—it is written about me in the scroll—I have come to do your will, O God" (Hebrews 10:7 NIV). He willingly completed the work He was sent to do, not for His own glory but in obedience to the Father. When He died, the curtain of the Holy of Holies was ripped in two, allowing you to enter into fellowship with a perfect God. The final sacrifice of His sinless body completely cleansed the stains of your past, present, and future mistakes.

Whereas Hebrew law required Old Testament Levitical priests to repeat the sin sacrifice year after year, Jesus' sacrifice erased the need to ever repeat any more sin offerings. "By one offering He has perfected for all time those who are sanctified" (Hebrews 10:14 NASB). Since you have been washed and purified by the blood of Christ, now you can do what the high priest could only symbolize—approach God with total confidence. Yet this doesn't mean you can sit around wallowing in a sinful lifestyle. God sent His son into the world because He loved you; obedience is your response to His love. Your love for Him should prompt you to offer yourself as a living sacrifice to God.

How do you do this? In Romans 12:2, Paul gives you some guidelines: "Do not conform any longer to the pattern of this world, but be transformed by the renewing of your mind" (NIV). In the same way that salmon swim upstream, you are to go against the flow of popular culture and distinguish yourself from the world by Christlike obedience. Jesus died once on the cross, but you must die every day to your sinful desires and temptations. True sacrifice can be painful, but in doing so, you bring God glory and become a hero of faith.

Jesus
The Perfect Sacrifice

What Matters Most...

◎ Jesus died for your sins so you don't have to. That's the good news.

◎ He conquered death and waits for you in heaven. You can count on it.

◎ Your conscience can be free of guilt. Jesus will take your burdens.

◎ Your life is a living sacrifice.

◎ Obedience is your response to His love.

What **Doesn't** Matter...

◎ Imitating the ways of the world. Go against the flow of pop culture.

◎ Trying to be perfect on your own. It's an impossible task. Don't even try it.

◎ Losing your life to save your soul. Give it all to Jesus.

◎ Expecting immediate transformation. Give yourself time to grow.

◎ Fearing what others will think. Focus only on what God thinks.

Focus Points...

He is the atoning sacrifice for our sins, and not for ours only but also for the sins of the whole world.
1 JOHN 2:2 NRSV

"Come now, let us reason together," says the LORD. "Though your sins are like scarlet, they shall be as white as snow."
ISAIAH 1:18 NIV

The sacrifice God wants is a broken spirit. God, you will not reject a heart that is broken and sorry for sin.
PSALM 51:17 NCV

What is more pleasing to the LORD: your burnt offerings and sacrifices or your obedience to his voice? Obedience is far better than sacrifice. Listening to Him is much better than offering the fat of rams.
1 SAMUEL 15:22 NLT

what really counts

I desire mercy and not sacrifice, and the knowledge of God more than burnt offerings.
HOSEA 6:6 NKJV

No man ever loved like Jesus ... He died on the cross to save us. And now God says, "Because He died, I can forgive you."
BILLY GRAHAM

Let us not forget that Christ laid down his life for us, and we in turn are to lay down our lives for each other.
ELISABETH ELLIOT

Jesus
At God's Right Hand

> There is one God, and one mediator also between God and men, the man Christ Jesus.
>
> 1 TIMOTHY 2:5 NASB

"He's MY baby!" "No, he's MINE!" Like cats in a brawl, two Hebrew women stood fighting over a tiny infant boy. They'd reached an impasse, where neither would give in. In desperation, they took their dispute to King Solomon. His response was simple: Take a sword and cut the baby in two, giving each woman half. Of course, the baby's real mother cried out in anguish, "Please, my Lord, give her the living baby! Don't kill him!" (1 Kings 3:26 NIV). In his wisdom, Solomon knew the real mother would give up her son rather than watch him die.

As a mediator, Solomon came in between the two dissenting mothers and brought peace.

In modern-day conference rooms, a mediator often goes between two parties who are in disagreement and seeks an amicable solution. This person bridges the gap that prevents reconciliation. Without a go-between, there would be only a great chasm of angry words and hurt feelings. A great breach also exists between humanity and holy God. All religions strive upward to reach God, but it is an impossible task. Only through the sacrifice of Jesus did God reach down to man and offer a solution of reconciliation. Jesus makes this very clear in John 14:6, when He says, "I am the way and the truth and the life. No one comes to the Father except through me" (NIV).

When Christ's work was done, He returned to heaven and sat down at God's right hand, but he's not just relaxing; he's constantly intervening on your behalf. He now serves as the High Priest who hears your prayers and intercedes for you. Scripture says, "For this reason Christ is the mediator of a new covenant, that those who are called may receive the promised eternal inheritance" (Hebrews 9:15 NIV). The Old Covenant didn't allow man to have fellowship with God without a sacrificial offering; with the New Covenant, Jesus was the permanent sacrifice.

Christ now serves as the living way for you to enter into the presence of God. You can offer your prayers in full confidence, knowing that God will accept them through the purification of Jesus' cleansing sacrifice. When you talk to God, your prayers are lifted up like the sweet smell of burning incense before Christ. He allows you to "draw near with a sincere heart in full assurance of faith" (Hebrews 10:22 NASB). For believers, a gap no longer exists.

Jesus
At God's Right Hand

What Matters Most...

◉ Confessing your sins to Christ. He accepts you as you are.

◉ Praying openly to Christ. Your prayers are lifted up as incense.

◉ Embracing the love of Christ. His mercy never ends.

◉ Sharing faithfully the truth of Christ. The lost world needs your message.

◉ Exhibiting the character of Christ. He is always watching you.

What **Doesn't** Matter...

◉ The taunts of the devil. He has already been defeated.

◉ The Old Covenant laws of reconciliation. They've been replaced.

◉ Your grudges against others who have wronged you. Let them go.

◉ Your good behavior. It still stinks without Jesus to intercede.

◉ The mysteries of heaven's glory. You'll find out one day.

Focus Points...

The LORD says to my Lord: "Sit at my right hand until I make your enemies a footstool for your feet."
PSALM 110:1 NIV

As a priest, Christ made a single sacrifice for sins, and that was it! Then he sat down right beside God.
HEBREWS 10:12 MSG

Because Jesus lives forever, he will never stop serving as priest. So he is able always to save those who come to God through him because he always lives, asking God to help them.
HEBREWS 7:24–25 NCV

I am the resurrection and the life; he who believes in me, though he die, yet shall he live.
JOHN 11:25 RSV

**what
really
counts**

I will do whatever you ask for in my name, so that the Father's glory will be shown through the Son.
JOHN 14:13 GNT

Jesus is the God whom we can approach without pride and before whom we can humble ourselves without despair.
BLAISE PASCAL

All that I am I owe to Jesus Christ, revealed to me in His divine Book.
DAVID LIVINGSTONE

What Matters Most to Me About
Jesus

Jesus took on human flesh and lived on earth. He experienced everything human beings experience and yet remained without sin. Now He sits at the right hand of God. Take some time to reflect on His life and work.

◉ *Philippians 2:1–11 describes how God humbled Himself to become the man, Jesus. He was obedient, even unto death. How can you make your life look more like that of Jesus?*

_____

_____

_____

_____

_____

_____

_____

_____

◉ *Do you remember a point in time when you realized Jesus was not some nice Sunday school character and that He was asking you for a commitment? Have you accepted Him as your Lord?*

_____

_____

_____

_____

_____

_____

_____

Jesus wept. He sweated. He groaned. He got angry. Now He sits in heaven, mediating on your behalf. What difference does that make in your life?

_____

_____

_____

_____

_____

_____

_____

_____

_____

Write a prayer to Jesus. What would you like to tell Him about the sacrifice He made on your behalf?

_____

_____

_____

_____

_____

_____

_____

_____

_____

He was God and man in one person, that God
and man might be happy together again.
GEORGE WHITEFIELD

HOLY SPIRIT

An Introduction

> This signet from God [the Holy Spirit] is the first installment on what's coming, a reminder that we'll get everything God has planned for us, a praising and glorious life.
>
> EPHESIANS 1:13–14 MSG

what really counts

There's a joke about a lumberjack who trades in his axe for a chain saw, having heard that this new-fangled contraption would enable him to cut down a hundred trees a day, but on his first day back in the woods, he only manages to cut down ten trees. Day after day he works himself into a lather, determined to cut down a hundred trees, but he never manages to fell more trees than he could have felled with his axe. Finally he gives up and takes the saw back to the store to see if there's something wrong with it. Not seeing any obvious problem, the salesman jerks the crank-cord and the saw roars to life. The lumberjack jumps ten feet in the air, and his eyes grow wide with wonder. "What's that noise?!" he gasps.

If you're in Christ, you have a source of incredible power in your life—much more powerful than any chain-saw engine. How surprised would you be if the Holy Spirit roared to life in your world? He is your Friend, your Comforter, your Teacher. He is God, and He lives in your life. Yet often Christians don't tap into that power, choosing instead to live a "Christian" life in their own efforts. When the Bible speaks of the Holy Spirit's power, the Greek word is *dunamis*. It's the word from which we get the word *dynamite*. The Holy Spirit's power is explosive power. It's the power to turn the world upside down!

Spirit-filled souls are ablaze for God. They love with a love that glows. They serve with a faith that kindles. They serve with a devotion that consumes.

SAMUEL CHADWICK

Holy Spirit
The Energizer

> I'll put my Spirit in you and make it
> possible for you to do what I tell you
> and live by my commands.
>
> EZEKIEL 36:27 MSG

what really counts

What inspires you? Maybe the story of an athlete who comes back from injury to take the gold at the Olympics. Or the story of the GIs who stormed the beaches at Normandy, giving all in the cause of freedom. The Bible, too, has its share of inspirational stories: Joseph pressing on through slavery and imprisonment to become Pharaoh's right-hand man and the savior of his people; David facing down Goliath; Daniel in the lions' den. Stories of human triumph, of dramatic comebacks and impossible odds have the power to inspire. They make you want to be braver, stand taller, love better.

But the real heart of Christianity is another kind of inspiration: the inspiration of the Holy Spirit. The word *inspire* literally means "to breathe into." The Holy Spirit, God Himself, is breathed into your life when you receive Christ. That is the power of God at work in your life—not figuratively, not metaphorically, but really. If inspirational stories

66

make you *want* to be better, the inspiration of the Holy Spirit literally gives you the *power* to be better. The power that raised Jesus from the dead is the power that triumphs over sin, and that power lives in you.

The Christian life isn't easy. God calls you to do things that you can't do on your own. You can't love your enemy in your own strength. You don't have enough willpower to keep the Ten Commandments—especially when Jesus says that to lust in your heart is to commit adultery and to hate your neighbor is to commit murder. You don't have it in you to be holy. If you try to do it in your own strength, you're either headed for spiritual burnout or the worst sort of self-righteousness, but there is good news. As Jesus told His disciples, "You will receive power when the Holy Spirit has come to you." You will have power to be everything God wants you to be. You will have the power, even, to "crush Satan under your feet" (Romans 16:20 NKJV).

Do you find the stories of the Bible inspiring? Remember that the same Holy Spirit who was at work in those stories is at work in your life too. For that matter, the same Holy Spirit who inspired the prophets and apostles to write the Bible is in you, speaking wisdom to you, interpreting the Scriptures. That's real inspiration. That's real power.

Holy Spirit
The Energizer

What Matters Most...

◎ Realizing that the Holy Spirit is God, and not just a warm feeling or a figure of speech.

◎ Recognizing that apart from the Holy Spirit you can't live the Christian life.

◎ Tapping into the explosive power that dwells within you.

◎ Understanding that this person is the same person who wrote the Bible, raised Lazarus from the dead, even created the world.

◎ Living a transformed life.

What **Doesn't** Matter...

◎ The old you. The Holy Spirit gives new life.

◎ Your weakness. The Holy Spirit gives strength.

◎ Your lack of knowledge. The Holy Spirit applies truth to your heart.

◎ Your reluctance to witness to others. The Holy Spirit gives you a holy boldness.

◎ Your spiritual coldness. The Holy Spirit is a warming fire.

Focus Points...

You are not ruled by your sinful selves. You are ruled by the Spirit, if that Spirit of God really lives in you ... God raised Jesus from the dead, and if God's Spirit is living in you, he will also give life to your bodies that die.
ROMANS 8:9, 11 NCV

When God is personally present, a living Spirit, that old, constricting legislation is recognized as obsolete. We're free of it!
2 CORINTHIANS 3:17 MSG

The church throughout Judea, Galilee, and Samaria had a time of peace. Through the help of the Holy Spirit it was strengthened and grew in numbers, as it lived in reverence for the Lord.
ACTS 9:31 GNT

what really counts

Work out your salvation with fear and trembling; for it is God who is at work in you, both to will and to work for His good pleasure.
PHILIPPIANS 2:12–13 NASB

May the Spirit's holy flame ignite in us for God's great name a holy passion, zeal and fire that magnify him with desire.
JOHN PIPER

If the Spirit of God detects anything in you that's wrong, He does not ask you to put it right; He asks you to accept the light, and he will put it right.
OSWALD CHAMBERS

Holy Spirit
Your Comforter

The true children of God are those who let God's Spirit lead them. The Spirit we received does not make us slaves again to fear; it makes us children of God. With that Spirit we cry out, "Father."

ROMANS 8:14–15 NCV

what really counts

Their last night with Jesus—the night before His crucifixion—the disciples were understandably upset. Jesus had been the best of friends to them, but now He said He was going away. "Let not your hearts be troubled," He soothed, but their hearts were still troubled. Jesus promised that He would prepare a place for them where He was going, but even that wasn't altogether comforting. Thomas, ever literal-minded and matter-of-fact, asked, "Lord, we do not know where You are going, and how can we know the way?" (John 14:5 NKJV). In retrospect, it seemed like a simplistic and unspiritual thing to say, but under the circumstances, it was actually a pretty good question. Without Jesus there to show them the way, how would any of them get to heaven?

So Jesus, Friend of sinners, promised a new friend who would pick up where He left off: "I will pray the Father, and He will give you another Helper, that He may abide with you forever—the Spirit of truth" (John 14:16–17 NKJV). The word translated "Helper" here is *paraklete,* literally "one who comes along beside." Sometimes it is translated "Comforter." In any case, He is a Companion, a divine Companion, who shows the way to heaven.

The Spirit of God is the Spirit of truth, and like any other faithful friend, He speaks truth into the life of a believer. Sometimes that truth is a word of encouragement, a reminder of who you are before God, as when "The Spirit Himself bears witness with our spirit that we are children of God" (Romans 8:16 NKJV). Other times, the Spirit speaks a harder truth, convicting you of sin and spurring you on to repentance. "When He has come, He will convict the world of sin, and of righteousness, and of judgment" (John 16:8 NKJV). Even then, your divine Companion seeks always to build up, never to tear down.

The Holy Spirit is not a theological abstraction. He is not a warm feeling, or an impersonal force, or a symbol or metaphor, like the Christmas spirit or school spirit or the Spirit of '76. Like God the Father and God the Son, God the Holy Spirit is a person—a person who desires to have fellowship with you. He is "a friend who sticks closer than a brother." That relationship is one of the great privileges of the Christian life.

Holy Spirit
Your Comforter

What Matters Most...

- Hearing the encouragement of the Holy Spirit. He speaks the truth.

- Responding to the conviction of the Holy Spirit. He bears witness.

- Resting in the comforts of the Holy Spirit. He comes to comfort you.

- Basking in the friendship of the Holy Spirit. He seeks to build you up.

- Speaking the truth of the Holy Spirit.

What Doesn't Matter...

- Discouraging words. The Holy Spirit is your encourager. A relationship with Him is a great privilege.

- Condemnation. Conviction comes from the Holy Spirit. Condemnation doesn't.

- Loneliness. The Holy Spirit is your divine Friend. And He is your divine companion.

- Feelings of inadequacy. The Holy Spirit is your help.

- Anxiety. The Holy Spirit is your comfort.

Focus Points...

Where can I go to get away from your Spirit? Where can I run from you? If I go up to the heavens, you are there. If I lie down in the grave, you are there.
PSALM 139:7–8 NCV

Do you not know that you are the temple of God and that the Spirit of God dwells in you?
1 CORINTHIANS 3:16 NKJV

May the God of hope fill you with all joy and peace in believing, that you may abound in hope by the power of the Holy Spirit.
ROMANS 15:13 NKJV

God affirms us, making us a sure thing in Christ, putting his Yes within us. By his Spirit he has stamped us with his eternal pledge—a sure beginning of what he is destined to complete.
2 CORINTHIANS 1:21–22 MSG

what really counts

What the church needs today is . . . men whom the Holy Ghost can use. The Holy Ghost does not flow through methods, but through men.

E. M. BOUNDS

O Holy Spirit, descend plentifully into my heart. Enlighten the dark corners of this neglected dwelling and scatter there Thy cheerful beams.

SAINT AUGUSTINE

What Matters Most to Me About
The Holy Spirit

People sometimes speak of the Holy Spirit as "it," as if the Holy Spirit lacked personhood. God the Holy Spirit is no less God than God the Father or God the Son. Any effort to understand the Holy Spirit and how He works in your life is effort well spent.

◎ *It is through the Holy Spirit that God's transforming power is translated into the lives of believers. How have you experienced that transformation in your own life or in the lives of others?*

_____

_____

_____

_____

what
really
counts _____

_____

_____

_____

_____

◎ *Where do you need to see the Holy Spirit's exploding power in your life? Why?*

_____

_____

_____

_____

_____

_____

◎ *Write about a time when the Holy Spirit brought comfort into your life.*

_____

_____

_____

_____

_____

_____

_____

_____

_____

_____

◎ *One role of the Holy Spirit is to shed light on passages of Scripture that are hard to understand. What's a passage you find difficult? Pray for the illumination of the Holy Spirit.*

_____

_____

_____

_____

_____

_____

_____

_____

_____

_____

Wise leaders should have known that the human heart cannot exist in a vacuum. Christ died for our hearts, and the Holy Spirit wants to come and satisfy them.

A. W. TOZER

FAITH

An Introduction

> Faith is the substance of things hoped for, the evidence of things not seen.
>
> HEBREWS 11:1 NKJV

what really counts

One of the most famous liars of the twentieth century was Joseph Goebbels. He was the Nazi Minister of Propaganda before and during World War II. It was his job to spread falsehood on behalf of Adolf Hitler.

If you asked any German in the 1930s or '40s whether or not he believed in Joseph Goebbels, you would have gotten a confident yes. Goebbels was a public figure, and his name was often in the papers. If you asked the same German whether or not he *believed* Goebbels, you might have gotten a different answer. Some believed his lies, some didn't. No doubt German Jews in particular doubted Goebbels, even though they couldn't help but believe *in* him.

Christian faith—saving faith—is about *believing* God, not about believing *in* Him. God cannot lie, and He accepts those who take Him at His word. Believing that God exists is a good start, but it isn't really faith. As the book of James says, even the demons believe in God, and shudder at the thought. That kind of belief doesn't do them any good. By contrast, "Abraham believed God, and it was accounted to him for righteousness" (James 2:23 NKJV). Abraham believed that God would do what He said He would do. He trusted God's faithfulness enough to rest his whole life and livelihood on that belief. That's what genuine faith looks like. It is more than an acknowledgment of God's existence. It is the soul's response to the utter faithfulness of God.

Love is the crowning grace in Heaven, but faith is the conquering grace upon earth.

THOMAS WATSON

Faith
Not by Works

> By grace you have been saved
> through faith, and that not of
> yourselves; it is the gift of God.
>
> EPHESIANS 2:8 NKJV

what really counts

If ever anyone had reason to trust in his own works for salvation, it was the apostle Paul. His Jewish credentials were impeccable. He wasn't just a law-abiding citizen; he was one of the Pharisees, Israel's religious Dream Team. He wasn't just obedient to the Jewish law; he was zealous for it, hotly persecuting Christians to their deaths. Within his religious tradition, he was unimpeachable, but Paul needed faith, not religion. He needed to put his confidence in what God had done, not in what he could do.

When Jesus Christ got hold of him, Paul realized how irrelevant his religiosity was. Worse than that, he viewed it as excrement: "Compared to the high privilege of knowing Christ Jesus as my Master, firsthand, everything I once thought I had going for me is insignificant—dog dung" (Philippians 3:8 MSG). Why was Paul so adamant—and so crude? Because all that self-righteousness kept him from laying hold of the righteousness of Christ. It almost cost him his soul. He desires only to "gain Christ and be found in Him, not having my own righteousness, which is from the law, but that which is through faith in Christ" (Philippians 3:8–9 NKJV).

If you want to be saved, you must turn away from your old ways, turn to Christ, and rest in His perfect work. You may be a crack-addicted bank robber. If so, then the gospel is simple: Turn from your wicked ways and cling to the cross of Christ, but if you're reading this book, there's a good chance you're nicer than that. You may be a family man. You may be a deacon. You may volunteer at the Humane Society. You may have to rack your brain to come up with any decent sins to repent of. If that's you, here's a question: Have you repented of your good works? Because those good works, if you're trusting in them to earn your way to God, will sink you just as fast as the sins of the vilest sinner.

The old hymn "Rock of Ages" says, "Nothing in my hand I bring. Simply to thy cross I cling." When you go to Christ, make sure your hands are empty. Because if you hold too tightly to any of your works, good or bad, you may not have a free hand to grab onto the only thing that can save you.

Faith
Not by Works

What Matters Most...

- The privilege of knowing Christ as Savior. It overshadows all religious accomplishments.

- The righteousness that comes through faith in Christ. It's the only righteousness you have.

- The cross of Christ. There's something you can safely glory in.

- The sufficiency of Christ. You don't have to add anything to His finished work.

- The Gift of God. Here is where your salvation begins and ends.

What Doesn't Matter...

- Your good works. If you're depending on them to make you right with God.

- Your bad deeds. Those are covered too.

- Your religiosity. If it causes you to put your confidence anywhere but Christ.

- Your reputation. If it distracts you from the centrality of Christ.

- Your zeal. If it's not motivated by a love for Christ and directed by the Holy Spirit.

Focus Points...

We know very well that we are not set right with God by rule-keeping but only through personal faith in Jesus Christ. How do we know? We tried it—and we had the best system of rules the world has ever seen! Convinced that no human being can please God by self-improvement, we believed in Jesus as the Messiah so that we might be set right before God by trusting in the Messiah, not by trying to be good.

GALATIANS 2:16 MSG

I bear them witness that they [the Israelites] have a zeal for God, but not according to knowledge. For they being ignorant of God's righteousness, and seeking to establish their own righteousness, have not submitted to the righteousness of God.

ROMANS 10:2–3 NKJV

what really counts

Faith is to believe what we do not see, and the reward of faith is to see what we believe.

SAINT AUGUSTINE

At the beginning of every act of faith, there is often a seed of fear. For great acts of faith are seldom born out of calm calculation.

MAX LUCADO

81

Faith

Faith in God, Not Faith in Faith

If we are faithless, He remains faithful; He cannot deny Himself.
2 TIMOTHY 2:13 NKJV

what really counts

The contrast must have been striking: A Roman centurion, tall and splendid in glittering armor stood before Jesus, who wore a simple, unadorned robe, no trappings of earthly power. Even more striking was the way the centurion, representative of the world's mightiest empire, addressed the Healer from Galilee. "Lord, my servant is lying paralyzed at home, fearfully tormented." Lord? He called Jesus Lord?

"I will come and heal him," Jesus answered, but the Roman wouldn't hear of it. "Lord, I am not worthy for you to come under my roof, but just say the word, and my servant will be healed. For I also am a man under authority, with soldiers under me; and I say to this one, 'Go!' and he goes, and to another, 'Come,' and he comes, and to my slave, 'Do this!' and he does it" (Matthew 8:6–9 NASB). A commander of men, the centurion knew how to get things done, but he found himself in a situation where there was nothing he could do.

He could order men to come and go, but he couldn't order the sickness to leave his servant. So he turned to the One who had authority even over sickness and death.

Jesus not only healed the centurion's servant, but He also marveled at the strength of the man's faith. It's worth noting how little religious language the centurion used. He didn't try to impress Jesus with God-talk. He didn't actually talk about faith; instead, he lived it. Just as importantly, the centurion didn't place faith in his own faith. He harbored no illusion that the strength of his faith was the key to healing his servant. The only strength he claimed was the strength of Jesus, who could order the sickness to leave. That's a picture of genuine faith: a simple act of trusting Jesus as the One who can get things done—things you could never do for yourself.

How strong is your faith? The question is a little misleading, for it makes it sound as if the measure of your faith is your capacity to believe or your ability to stave off disbelief.

The important thing about faith isn't the strength of your faith, but the strength of the God in whom you place your faith. Faith the size of a mustard seed is sufficient, as long as that faith if placed in the God who moves mountains.

Faith
Faith in God, Not Faith in Faith

What Matters Most...

- ◎ God's faithfulness. He always does what He says He will do.

- ◎ God's power. He can do all things. God is all powerful and almighty.

- ◎ God's goodness. He delights to reward the faithful.

- ◎ Simple trust. It's enough to know, "I am weak, but he is strong."

- ◎ The willingness to ask. Bring your troubles to the God, who heals.

What **Doesn't** Matter...

- ◎ Your faithlessness. Even when you're faithless, God is faithful.

- ◎ The seeming impossibility of your circumstances. Place your concerns in God's hands.

- ◎ Your weakness. God's strength is made perfect in weakness.

- ◎ Your challenges. All things are possible with God.

- ◎ Your waning confidence. Place your confidence in the unfailing God.

Focus Points...

The blind men came up to Him, and Jesus said to them, "Do you believe that I am able to do this?" They said to Him, "Yes, Lord." Then He touched their eyes, saying, "It shall be done to you according to your faith." And their eyes were opened.
MATTHEW 9:28–30 NASB

God is not man, one given to lies, and not a son of man changing his mind. Does he speak and not do what he says? Does he promise and not come through?
NUMBERS 23:19 MSG

Jesus said to him, . . . "All things are possible to him who believes." Immediately the boy's father cried out and said, "I do believe; help my unbelief."
MARK 9:23–24 NASB

what really counts

It is not great faith, but true faith, that saves; and the salvation lies, not in the faith, but in the Christ in whom faith trusts . . . Surely a man can believe what he knows to be true; and as you know Jesus to be true, you, my friend, can believe in Him.

CHARLES SPURGEON

Faith is the art of holding on to things your reason has once accepted in spite of your changing moods.

C. S. LEWIS

85

What Matters Most to Me About
Faith

Faith is as simple as believing that God is going to do what He has said He will do. Yet it plays itself out in thousands of ways, in thousands of daily choices.

◎ *Even if you believe that all of God's promises are true, there's usually at least one area of you life where fears keep you from fully living out God's promises. Do you have such an area? Write about it.*

_____

_____

_____

_____

_____

what
really
counts

_____

_____

_____

◎ *Now write a prayer asking God to give you more faith in that area.*

_____

_____

_____

_____

_____

_____

_____

Think of a time in your life when you made a choice by faith, something that went against earthly reason. How did God reward that faith?

_____

_____

_____

_____

_____

_____

_____

_____

_____

Nothing builds your faith like reflecting on the faithfulness of God. Write about a time when you've seen God keep a biblical promise in your life.

_____

_____

_____

_____

_____

_____

_____

_____

_____

_____

God will honor our faith.

DWIGHT L. MOODY

LOVE

An Introduction

> This is my command: Love one another the way I loved you.
>
> JOHN 15:12 MSG

what really counts

Love is a word that is used to mean so many different things, it sometimes seems to mean nothing. Add to that the fact that people often use *love* to mean something that's not love at all, and it's not easy to come up with a useful and comprehensive definition of the word. C. S. Lewis offers up a good effort: "Love is not affectionate feeling, but a steady wish for the loved person's ultimate good as far as it can be obtained." Of course, love often—perhaps usually—entails affectionate feelings, but as Lewis suggests, those feelings don't define love. The real defining characteristic of love is a certain steadiness of purpose.

It helps to think in those terms—love as the workmanlike, matter-of-fact pursuit of someone else's good. It weeds out a good many impostors, such as infatuation and the using of other people. At the same time, it draws some of the quieter, less dramatic kinds of love closer to the center—the love of a nursing home worker for her patients, the love of an army unit commander for his men.

That definition of *love* leaves something out: the happiness of the one who loves. Sacrificial love often doesn't feel like a sacrifice when everything is totaled up, for the rewards of genuine love outweigh its costs. When you realize that lasting happiness is to be found in making someone else genuinely happy, the doors to real love and real happiness swing wide.

> The wonderful thing about Christianity is that it not only tells us to do the loving thing, it also tells us what that loving thing is.
>
> JOSH MCDOWELL

Love
An Act of the Will

> Never let a problem to be solved
> become more important than a
> person to be loved.
> BARBARA JOHNSON

what really counts

Consider what happens when a couple goes to an orphanage to adopt a child. The place is full of children, one as unfamiliar to the adopting couple as the next. As they walk through the dormitory they look into each little face and wonder, "Is this our child?" At last the orphanage keeper presents their child to them. In that moment they decide, whether consciously or unconsciously, "this is the child we will love as our own." They have chosen to love her. It won't be very long before they don't even realize that it had been a choice.

People often think of love as a feeling. If you ask those parents about their new daughter, they will no doubt tell you how they feel about her, but those feelings are only one aspect of their love. There's also the choice that gave rise to those feelings. That choice also gives rise to actions—actions that aim to benefit the people you love. C. S. Lewis wrote, "Do not waste time bothering whether you 'love' your neighbour; act as if you did. As soon as we do this we find one of the great secrets. When you are behaving as if you loved someone, you will presently come to love him." It's almost as if the good feelings are the reward for the good decision.

The Bible repeatedly commands the godly to love others. If you think of love as a feeling, that doesn't make sense. You can't command people to feel things. You can only command them to choose and to do. It's worth noting that there are two main Greek words that are translated as *love*. *Phileo* describes the feeling of love—affection, you might say. *Agapao,* or *agape,* on the other hand, describes love as an action or a choice. The New Testament uses both words. Paul, for instance frequently speaks of the *phileo,* or affection, he feels for the Christians he's writing to, but every time there is a command to love, the writer uses *agapao* rather than *phileo*. That is to say, the Bible doesn't command you to *feel* love. It commands you to *do* love.

That's not to say, however, that love is a chore. It's a choice, even a responsibility, but it's a responsibility that carries its own reward. The more you love, the more love you feel. That's truly rewarding.

Love
An Act of the Will

What Matters Most...

◎ The decision to love. It's your choice. Deciding to love is an act of will.

◎ Acting on your love. Real love has legs. And you have many opportunities.

◎ Steadiness of purpose. Keep plodding. Persistence will be rewarded.

◎ God's love for you. There's your motivation for loving others.

◎ Faith, hope, love. What matters most is love.

What **Doesn't** Matter...

◎ The return on your love. Sometimes you aren't loved back; and that's okay.

◎ The ebb and flow of affectionate feelings. That's natural.

◎ Other people's unlovableness. Make the decision to love anyway. Loved people often become more lovable.

◎ The risk of loving. The rewards outweigh the risks.

◎ Your rough edges. They're no excuse not to love.

Focus Points...

The most important command is this: "Listen, people of Israel! The Lord our God is the only Lord. Love the Lord your God with all your heart, all your soul, all your mind, and all your strength." The second command is this: "Love your neighbor as you love yourself." There are no commands more important than these.

MARK 12:29–31 NCV

Hope does not disappoint, because the love of God has been poured out in our hearts by the Holy Spirit who was given to us.

ROMANS 5:5 NKJV

Love from the center of who you are; don't fake it. Run for dear life from evil; hold on for dear life to good.

ROMANS 12:9 MSG

what really counts

These three things continue forever: faith, hope, and love. And the greatest of these is love.

1 CORINTHIANS 13:13 NCV

There is a time for risky love. There is a time for extravagant gestures. There is a time to pour out your affections on one you love. And when the time comes—seize it, don't miss it.

MAX LUCADO

Whoever loves much, does much.

THOMAS À KEMPIS

Love
Loving Well

Love suffers long and is kind; love does not envy;
love does not parade itself, is not puffed up; does
not behave rudely, does not seek its own.

1 CORINTHIANS 13:4–5 NKJV

When the movie *Casablanca* begins, Humphrey Bogart's
character Rick is a hard man. He seems impervious to all
human emotion, aloof from all entanglements, but he begins
to change when Ilsa shows up in Casablanca. She's the only
person Rick has ever loved, and her arrival opens him back up
to the painful tenderness that he had hoped to escape when
he came to this remote corner of the world. Perhaps he could
love again, be happy again. Except that Ilsa is married to
another man: Viktor Lazslo, a leader of the Czech Resistance
against the Nazis.

In the movie's final scene, Rick shows the true nature of
his love. Ilsa's husband's life is in danger, and Rick is in a position to get him out of Nazi-controlled Casablanca. Ilsa offers
to leave Viktor and stay with Rick if only he will save her husband's life. There's nothing Rick would like better than for
Ilsa to stay, but he knows she has a key role to play in the fight

against the Nazis; and he knows that she belongs with the man she married. So when the plane leaves Casablanca, Rick makes sure both Viktor and Ilsa are on it. He lays aside his own agenda for Ilsa's life so that she will be free to pursue a higher purpose.

Sometimes men feel a sort of ownership over the people they love—as if love were a license to control their loved ones. To love another person well is not to impose your own plan on their life, but rather to help them live out the purposes that God has for them. The choices aren't usually as stark as Rick's in *Casablanca*. Usually the choices are much smaller and quieter. You decide not to manipulate your wife into "choosing" what you wanted all along. You let your son play soccer even though you always wanted a football star in the family. You encourage a friend at work to go after a better job opportunity, even though it means one less buddy at the water cooler.

When you love somebody, sometimes it's hard to resist imposing your plan on them. You love them, after all, so what you want for them must be best, right? But loving another person sometimes calls for sacrifice—and the humility to know that it's not you, but God, who has the perfect plan for their life.

Love
Loving Well

What Matters Most...

◉ Submitting to God's plan for your loved ones' lives. He knows what is best.

◉ Being willing to sacrifice.

◉ Refusing to manipulate your loved ones. Make a conscious effort to respect their decisions.

◉ Asking what you can give, not what you can get.

◉ Being creative. It takes imagination to love well.

What **Doesn't** Matter...

◉ Your natural selfishness. Overcome it. Selfishness doesn't pay.

◉ Your plan for your loved ones' lives. God's plan is better.

◉ Other people's motives. It's hard enough to know your own.

◉ The habit of using people. With the help of the Holy Spirit, you can break that pattern.

◉ The fear of losing a loved one if you loosen your grip. It's a chance you take when you love well.

Focus Points...

Let nothing be done through selfish ambition or conceit, but in lowliness of mind let each esteem others better than himself. Let each of you look out not only for his own interests, but also for the interests of others.
PHILIPPIANS 2:3–4 NKJV

Greater love has no one than this, than to lay down one's life for his friends.
JOHN 15:13 NKJV

Husbands, love your wives as Christ loved the church and gave himself for it.
EPHESIANS 5:25 NCV

You can't go wrong when you love others. When you add up everything in the law code, the sum total is love.
ROMANS 13:10 MSG

what really counts

Most importantly, love each other deeply, because love will cause many sins to be forgiven.
1 PETER 4:8 NCV

Whom you would change, you must first love.
OSWALD CHAMBERS

Love has a hem to her garment that reaches the very dust. It sweeps the streets and lanes, and because it can, it must.
MOTHER TERESA

What Matters Most to Me About
Love

Love is a word used to mean many different things. Perhaps the most reliable meaning is that of simply putting another person's interests ahead of your own. Spend some time reflecting on the role of love in your life.

◎ *Whom do you have a really hard time loving? What can you do to demonstrate the love of Christ?*

_____

_____

_____

_____

_____

_____

_____

_____

◎ *Think about some of the people you love the most. How is your love for them active, reaching out, seeking their best interest? Or is your love just a response to their loveliness?*

_____

_____

_____

_____

_____

_____

_____

what
really
counts

○ *What's in it for you? How has your life been enriched by loving other people?*

_____

_____

_____

_____

_____

_____

_____

_____

_____

○ *Think about a time when you were the recipient of love that you didn't deserve. How did that make a difference in your life?*

_____

_____

_____

_____

_____

_____

_____

_____

If love is the path of fullest joy, then let us pray for the power to love "that our joy might be full!"

JOHN PIPER

HEAVEN

An Introduction

> God will wipe away every tear from their eyes; there shall be no more death, nor sorrow, nor crying. There shall be no more pain, for the former things have passed away.
>
> REVELATION 21:4 NKJV

what really counts

A traveler drops his carry-on to embrace his wife. Her eyes glisten with tears of joy to see him safely home again. The fear and uncertainty in a little girl's face melt away when she catches sight of her grandparents waiting to welcome her after a long and lonesome flight. The airport is a place of joyful reunions. Perhaps it is a preview of heaven.

Heaven, according to the songwriter Billy Sprague, is one long hello. On earth there is always something to say good-bye to. Friends move away. Loved ones die. All good things come to an end. The joy of meeting a loved one after a long absence is a little glimpse of heaven, the eternal hello.

Almost from the start, the story of the human race has been one of separation and loss. Adam and Eve's disobedience got them kicked out of Eden and separated from God. It brought tears and hardship and death, but heaven repairs all that. There will be no more death, no more sorrow. God will wipe away every tear. He will dwell with His people, who on earth suffered separation from Him.

Heaven so far exceeds the human imagination that it's hard even to talk about it. How do you picture an eternal hello? The best you can do sometimes is to talk about what isn't there—no more sorrow, no more death, no more tears. No more loss or separation. That's what you have to look forward to.

> Death ... is no more than passing from one room into another, but there's a difference for me, you know. Because in that other room, I shall be able to see.
>
> HELEN KELLER

Heaven
Your Deepest Longing

> He has planted eternity in the human heart,
> but even so, people cannot see the whole
> scope of God's work from beginning to end.
> ECCLESIASTES 3:11 NLT

what really counts

You may have heard the old quip: Women use the remote control to find out what's on television; men use the remote control to find out what *else* is on television. Having a hundred channels doesn't seem to make it any easier to find something good to watch. It only gives you more reason to suspect that there's something better than the show you happen to be watching at any given moment.

That's how life on this earth feels sometimes. Whatever you're doing, whatever stage of life you're in, you always suspect there's something else that would give you greater happiness, deeper satisfaction. The human mind is always turning toward the next thing, hoping something better is just around the corner. You work yourself half to death for a promotion, but it doesn't take long before the shine is off that new job and you start looking toward the *next* promotion. That new truck is great, but you've barely pulled the sticker off the window before you realize that what you really want is a boat to pull behind it.

Much of that, obviously, is just plain ambition and materialism, but on some fundamental level, the longing for something else, something better, is just part of being human. Sure, human desires are often misguided, but your deepest longings, even when you don't realize it, are longings after God. You were made for heaven, not for earth, and the things of earth will always leave you wanting something more. Even if you get it right—even if you "set your affections on things above," as the apostle Paul put it—you still find yourself longing after something you cannot yet possess in full. This side of heaven, there will always be a gap between where you are and where you want to be.

In heaven, that gap will be closed. Fulfillment and happiness won't be just around the corner; you will have turned that corner. There you will find what you have been looking for. You will find the God who was your desire all along. The important thing about heaven isn't streets of gold or crystal seas or harp music. The important thing about heaven is that you will be present with God. There will be no more need to flip the channels looking for something better. You'll have nothing else to wait for. You'll have nowhere else to be.

Heaven
Your Deepest Longing

What Matters Most...

◎ Eternity. Take the long view.

◎ Being present with God. That's your goal and your destiny.

◎ Your deepest longings. Let them point you toward God.

◎ Patience. Keep holding out for the final milestone that matters most.

◎ Trust. It's hard to believe in what you can't see, but Jesus is waiting for you in a real place.

What Doesn't Matter...

◎ Earthly treasures. They can rot, rust, or be stolen, so set your heart on treasures that last forever.

◎ The next big thing. Live here and now, with one eye toward heaven.

◎ Lack of contentment. You can never expect to be perfectly fulfilled until you can finally rest in heaven.

◎ Self-actualization. Keep your focus on God, not on pop psychology that's based on human ideas.

◎ Knowing all the answers. The great news is, you don't have to understand everything right now.

Focus Points...

From now on there is reserved for me the crown of righteousness, which the Lord, the righteous judge, will give me
on that day, and not only to me but also to all who have
longed for his appearing.
2 TIMOTHY 4:8 NRSV

God made a promise to us, and we are waiting for a new
heaven and a new earth where goodness lives.
2 PETER 3:13 NCV

In this tent we groan, longing to be clothed with our heavenly dwelling.
2 CORINTHIANS 5:2 NRSV

This is what the Son promised to us—life forever.
1 JOHN 2:25 NCV

what really counts

Not everyone who calls me "Lord, Lord" will enter the kingdom of heaven, but only those who do what my Father in
heaven wants them to do.
MATTHEW 7:21 GNT

It is glorious to be far out on the ocean of divine love,
believing in God, and steering for Heaven straight away by
the direction of the Word of God.

CHARLES SPURGEON

One short sleep past, we wake eternally, and death shall be
no more; death, thou shalt die.

JOHN DONNE

Heaven
The Weight of Glory

> Momentary, light affliction is producing for us an eternal weight of glory far beyond all comparison.
>
> 2 CORINTHIANS 4:17 NASB

The Great Divorce, by C. S. Lewis, tells the story of a bus trip to heaven. When the narrator first steps off the bus, he is struck by the sheer size of the place. The spot where he stands is so big it makes the solar system seem like "an indoor sort of place." It's a place of great natural beauty, too, with grass and trees and flowers more vibrant than anything on earth. When the narrator bends down to pluck a daisy, however, he finds that he cannot break or even bend the stem, no matter how hard he tries. It's diamond hard. He tries to pick up a little leaf from the ground, but it's all he can do to budge it; it feels as heavy as a sack of coal.

The Great Divorce is a fantasy, of course, but this scene makes an important point about the biblical idea of heaven: It is a solid and substantial place—the kind of place that makes the things of earth seem less than real. Usually when you see heaven depicted in pictures or cartoons or movies, everything is soft and gauzy, airy and fluffy and white. People fly and float and strum harps. You wonder how anybody could stand to live in such a place for an eternity. In the popular imagination, heaven isn't nearly as solid as earth.

The Bible offers a very different picture. The things of earth—and its sufferings—are light and momentary. The glories of heaven are not only eternal, but weighty, heavy. If that realization sinks in, it changes the way you think about everything. It is always tempting to choose what gives pleasure or avoids pain in the short term. The Bible calls you to take the long view, the heavenly view. In the end, it will be the things of earth that look flimsy and insubstantial.

If you are in Christ, you are destined to be a man of substance. You are destined to be more real, more solid than this world could ever make you. From where you stand, the world and its trials look pretty solid and weighty, but you are headed toward a world that's even weightier, more solid. That's a source of great hope. You will experience disappointment, even suffering in this life; but the heaviness you experience here will all seem light as a feather someday, next to the solid joys and lasting pleasures of heaven.

Heaven
The Weight of Glory

What Matters Most...

◎ The big picture. Earth is just a small corner of reality.

◎ Solidity. You find true solidity in heaven.

◎ Glory. The things of earth seem dim next to the glories of heaven.

◎ Hope. You have a lot to look forward to

◎ The real you. You were made for heaven.

What **Doesn't** Matter...

◎ Light, momentary sufferings. Compared to heaven's glories, earth's difficulties will seem very small.

◎ Discouragement. You have reason to hope. Heaven holds many promises.

◎ Frustrations. Everything will be made right someday. Be patient.

◎ Boredom. Don't lose heart, but keep pressing toward the goal.

◎ Doubt. Everything will make sense someday. You don't have to understand it all now.

Focus Points...

Now we see a dim reflection, as if we were looking into a mirror, but then we shall see clearly. Now I know only a part, but then I will know fully, as God has known me.
1 CORINTHIANS 13:12 NCV

What we suffer now is nothing compared to the glory he will give us later.
ROMANS 8:18 NLT

Thus says the LORD: "Heaven is My throne, and earth is My footstool."
ISAIAH 66:1 NKJV

Rejoice and be exceedingly glad, for great is your reward in heaven.
MATTHEW 5:12 NKJV

what really counts

Oh come, let us worship and bow down; let us kneel before the LORD our Maker.
PSALM 95:6 NKJV

The best we can hope for in this life is a knothole peek at the shining realities ahead. Yet a glimpse is enough.
JONI EARECKSON TADA

Aim at heaven and you will get earth thrown in. Aim at earth and you will get neither.
C. S. LEWIS

What Matters Most to Me About
Heaven

Although it may seem like the earth is your home, you're heading a little bit closer to your everlasting residence every day. What are your thoughts on heaven?

⊙ *Isaiah 66:1 describes heaven as God's throne and earth as His footstool. Look all around you. How does that Scripture make you feel different about your life on earth?*

_____

_____

_____

_____

_____

_____

_____

_____

⊙ *What are some ideas you have about what life will be like in heaven? What are the main influences that helped shape your ideas?*

_____

_____

_____

_____

_____

_____

_____

⊙ *How does a person enter into heaven? Do you feel confident that you will have an open invitation? Why or why not?*

_____

_____

_____

_____

_____

_____

_____

_____

_____

⊙ *What is the first question you'd like to ask God when you enter into heaven?*

_____

_____

_____

_____

_____

_____

_____

_____

_____

How sweet is rest after fatigue! How sweet
will heaven be when our journey is ended.
GEORGE WHITEFIELD

GOD'S WORD

An Introduction

> Every word of God is flawless; he is a shield to those who take refuge in him.
>
> PROVERBS 30:5 NIV

what really counts

The how-to shelves at your local bookstore sag under the weight of ever more specific books on every topic you can imagine. How to lose weight and feel great. How to make a million dollars in worm farming. How to repair Chevy trucks (year models 1989–1997). You need information, advice, and inspiration to get by in this very complicated world. How-to and self-improvement books can provide valuable help in that regard, but you also need something that's more fundamental than the advice and techniques you get in books and magazines. You need a standard by which to judge what help is really helpful.

The Bible is a how-to book: how to glorify God and enjoy Him forever. It offers advice and guidance for every area of a godly life. That advice usually comes in the form of principles rather than techniques. The Bible has nothing to say about IRAs and 401(k)s, but it has plenty to say about your attitude toward your money and possessions. The Bible doesn't offer up a top-ten list of kid-friendly vacation spots, but it does provide a clear picture of a father's responsibilities toward his children.

In a changing world, techniques change. The Bible is about those truths that do not change. New ideas are coming at you from every direction. How do you discern what to listen to and what to ignore? If you are steeped in the Word of God, you are ready to make sense of any new idea or technique that might come your way.

> Those who walk in truth walk in liberty.
> BETH MOORE

God's Word
Sure Thing

> The grass withers, the flower fades, when the breath of the LORD blows upon it; surely the people are grass. The grass withers, the flower fades, but the word of our God stands forever.
>
> ISAIAH 40:7–8 NASB

what really counts

If you were to pick up a copy of the *Wall Street Journal* from twenty years ago, it would make for interesting reading. You might read of high-flying companies that don't even exist anymore. You might notice a few nuggets of "conventional wisdom" that have since been totally discredited. Perhaps you would be struck by the idea that the more things change, the more things stay the same. But there's one thing you'd better not do with an old newspaper: You'd better not flip to the stock listings and invest your nest egg based on the prices you see there.

You have data flying at you like water from a fire hydrant, but data always changes. That's why it keeps coming—because yesterday's data is no good anymore and has to be replaced with new. It can be a little disorienting, but truth doesn't change. The Bible was written two millennia ago and more, but it is as true and relevant today as it ever was. The

Word of God stands forever. Human beings don't. They fade away like grass. Human words and human information are even more temporary. They are always subject to error. Only the Word of God is sufficient to build a life on.

Jesus preached that the person who listens to His words, the Word of God, is like a man who builds his house on a foundation of solid rock. Storms come, the wind blows, the water rises, but the house stands firm. On the other hand, the life that is built on any foundation besides the Word of God is like a house built on the sand. It isn't as firm as it looks; any storm might be the one that causes it to collapse or float away.

There is a lot of uncertainty in this world. One thing you can be sure of is that storms will blow in your life. You need to be sure of more than that. What foundation is your life built on? On a day-to-day basis, what shapes your life more—the Word of God, or the newspaper? Maybe the structure and guidance in your life come from inter-office memos, but data changes. Policies change. The news is always something new, but the truths of the Word of God give you a solid place to stand, alongside believers from throughout the ages who have always found it true.

God's Word
Sure Thing

What Matters Most...

- ◎ Consistency. God's Word never changes. What was true in times past is still true.

- ◎ Relevance. The Bible is as relevant today as it ever was. Consider history and current events.

- ◎ History. For thousands of years, people have found God's Word to be true.

- ◎ A firm foundation. God's Word is a solid rock. You can be confident of that.

- ◎ Strength. You can stand firm in God's truth.

What Doesn't Matter...

- ◎ Life's storms. You can weather them if your life is built on the solid rock.

- ◎ Conventional wisdom. Human wisdom is always changing.

- ◎ Human error. God's Word is true.

- ◎ Uncertainty. God's Word is sure.

- ◎ The latest fads. You need the solidity of timeless truth.

Focus Points...

Man shall not live by bread alone; but man lives by every word that proceeds from the mouth of the LORD.
DEUTERONOMY 8:3 NKJV

In the beginning there was the Word. The Word was with God, and the Word was God.
JOHN 1:1 NCV

Take these words of mine to heart and keep them in mind. Write them down, tie them around your wrist, and wear them as headbands as a reminder.
DEUTERONOMY 11:18 GOD'S WORD

"Isn't my Message like fire?" GOD's Decree. "Isn't it like a sledgehammer busting a rock?"
JEREMIAH 23:29 MSG

The words of the LORD are pure words, like silver tried in a furnace of earth, purified seven times.
PSALM 12:6 NKJV

The word of God hidden in the heart is a stubborn voice to suppress.

BILLY GRAHAM

Go to the Bible to meet Christ ... He is its author, its subject matter, the doorway to its treasures, the full-throated symphony of which Adam and the prophets heard just the faintest tune.

ANDRE SEU

God's Word
Be Transformed

> Do not be conformed to this world, but be transformed by the renewing of your mind, that you may prove what is that good and acceptable and perfect will of God.
>
> ROMANS 12:2 NKJV

For forty days the giant Goliath spewed curses and challenges across the valley at the army of Israel. Every day they heard his taunts they grew a little weaker. The giant loomed larger in their eyes, and the truth of God's promises seemed a little further away. The Israelites were God's chosen people. Time and time again, God had delivered them in the face of impossible odds. The Israelite soldiers knew this. Yet the Philistine giant bent them to his will. He imposed his worldview on a whole army of people who should have known better.

Then came David. Maybe he was too innocent or idealistic to realize that sometimes people who talk about God's Word and God's promises don't actually have faith enough to trust in them. David, like his fellow Israelites, had always been taught that God was Israel's Deliverer, and he believed it. He believed it enough to go face the champion of the Philistines armed with nothing more than a sling and stones. He believed the Word of God more than he believed the "facts" of an impossible situation. He refused to listen to the threats of an enemy or to conform to the sheep-like fear of his compatriots. He changed history.

The promises of God are opened to you, too, in the Bible. The world is constantly trying to conform you to itself, to shape you in its own image. Perhaps it has already succeeded in some parts of your life, but God, through His Word, is able to transform you by renewing your mind. A new mind—a new way of thinking. That's the promise of God's Word. Do you believe God's promises more than you believe your circumstances? Has your mind been renewed in the Word so that you can go forward boldly while those around you are shrinking in fear?

The story of David and Goliath is more than just a story of victory in the face of long odds. It's a story of what happens when a man's mind is renewed by the promises of God. The conformists in the Israelite army came very close to letting themselves and their nation be destroyed. David, the young non-conformist, knew that God had something different in mind. God used him. Strange and wonderful things happen when people conform themselves to God's promises rather than letting themselves be conformed to the world around them.

God's Word
Be Transformed

What Matters Most...

◎ Transformation. The Word of God gives you a new mind.

◎ Boldness. The Word of God takes away the fear of men.

◎ Belief. The Word of God is truer than your circumstances.

◎ God's promises. He always keeps them.

◎ God's faithfulness. He is always faithful, even when you doubt.

What Doesn't Matter...

◎ Conformity. God has a better plan. You don't have to be like anyone else but yourself.

◎ Your weakness. The Word of God offers strength.

◎ Your fear. The Bible offers hope. There is nothing you can't handle with God by your side.

◎ Peer pressures. You answer to a higher authority. It doesn't really matter what other people do.

◎ The easy way out. Conformity to the world seems like the easy way, but in the end it isn't.

Focus Points...

Break open your words, let the light shine out, let ordinary people see the meaning.
PSALM 119:130 MSG

Be doers of the word, and not merely hearers who deceive themselves.
JAMES 1:22 NRSV

I have never left the commands he has spoken; I have treasured his words more than my own.
JOB 23:12 NCV

Your word I have treasured in my heart, that I may not sin against You.
PSALM 119:11 NASB

No, the word is very near you; it is in your mouth and in your heart so you may obey it.
DEUTERONOMY 30:14 NIV

what really counts

God's word is a light not only to our path but to our thinking. Place it in your heart today, and you will never walk in darkness.

JONI EARECKSON TADA

The study of God's word, for the purpose of discovering God's will, is the secret discipline which has formed the greatest characters.

J. W. ALEXANDER

What Matters Most to Me About
God's Word

Knowing God through His Word takes time and energy, just like any other relationship that matters to you. Whenever you read it, God can send you a personal message of guidance, comfort, encouragement, or warning.

◎ *Do you enjoy reading the Bible? Why or why not?*

_____

_____

_____

_____

_____

_____

_____

_____

◎ *God can arrange for you to read a specific passage on the very day you need to hear it. Have you ever felt like God spoke directly to you using a certain Scripture that you really needed to hear?*

_____

_____

_____

_____

_____

_____

_____

what
really
counts

◉ *James compares God's Word to a mirror (see James 1:23–25). In what ways is this true? How does seeing yourself in a real mirror compare to seeing yourself in God's Word?*

_____

_____

_____

_____

_____

_____

_____

_____

_____

◉ *Do you have a life verse, one that you would like to meditate on every day of your life? If not, use this space to write one down that is especially meaningful to you.*

_____

_____

_____

_____

_____

_____

_____

_____

_____

The life of faith says, "Lord, You have said it, it appears to be irrational, but I'm going to step out boldly, trusting in Your Word."
OSWALD CHAMBERS

The Future

An Introduction

> The mind of man plans his way, but the LORD directs his steps.
>
> PROVERBS 16:9 NASB

what really counts

Being a responsible man sometimes makes you feel like the weight of the world rests squarely on your shoulders. Your family trusts that you'll protect them and meet their physical and emotional needs. Your work obligations keep you occupied throughout the day, and even when you're home, you still have a few items simmering on your mind's back burner. Then there are church and community responsibilities that fill up your nights and weekends. If you could only see into the future, you'd know where to best invest your time.

Since it's impossible to predict what will happen tomorrow, much less a year from now, your best bet is to stay focused on what matters most. God's in charge of the future, and He doesn't want you to worry about what will happen. We're commanded to simply "fix our eyes on Jesus, the author and perfecter of our faith" (Hebrews 12:2 NIV). He's not going anywhere. Though you may wake up tomorrow and find that your company has outsourced or downsized you out of a job, you still have Someone who is in charge.

If God has enough power and energy to raise the sun and cause it to set, he's got your life under His ultimate control. He wants you to relax in His wisdom. Civil engineer Charles C. Noble said, "You must have long-range goals to keep you from being frustrated by short-range failures." Your main goal is to please God and serve Him, and if you're making Him your first priority, He's not going to let you go.

> The best thing about the future is that it only comes one day at a time.
>
> ABRAHAM LINCOLN

The Future
In God's Hands

Scripture says: "No eye has seen, no ear has heard, and no mind has imagined the things that God has prepared for those who love him."
1 CORINTHIANS 2:9 GOD'S WORD

what really counts

With the technology available these days, you may find yourself aware of more information than you ever thought possible. The Internet and 24-hour cable allow you to see global events unfolding almost as if they were taking place in your backyard. No longer do you only hear just your local weather forecast; instead, you're aware of every possible storm brewing on the entire planet. You know where the latest terrorist attack occurred almost as soon as it happens. Every time a company lays off employees, you immediately know how many, and it may cause you to wonder how much longer you'll be able to keep your own job.

It can be tempting to let all this knowledge fill you with fears about the future. Newspaper columnists and talk show hosts make their livings predicting what they believe will happen next, but Jesus was wise when He told His followers, "Do not worry about tomorrow, for tomorrow will worry about itself. Each day has enough trouble of its own" (Matthew 6:34 NIV). God's big enough to wrap Himself around the world, and the future is in His hands. His big plan for your life will unfold gradually, as you remain faithful to the tasks before you, step by step.

Every day, young men and women enter military academies and the armed forces in the hopes that they'll make a difference in protecting their country. In August 2001, as freshmen entered academies, they had no idea that a month later, our country would be under attack, and their training would possibly lead them into the war against terrorism. Parents who have children serving in the armed forces must live with the fear that their sons or daughters may face grave danger as part of duty, but that's where faith can root in to build up hope.

You don't know what the next five, ten, or a hundred years hold, but you do know who is in control and where your eternal destination will be if you put your trust in Christ. Matthew Henry once said, "God has wisely kept us in the dark concerning future events and reserved for himself the knowledge of them, that he may train us up in a dependence upon himself." Just as you need daily food to keep you physically nourished, Jesus wants you to depend on him to feed your faith. He'll enable you to face the unknown future with great hope.

The Future
In God's Hands

What Matters Most...

◎ Keeping your eyes focused on truth, not on what everyone is trying to predict.

◎ Pressing on when you feel like you've lost hope and want to give up.

◎ Trusting God that He has a plan that is for your ultimate good.

◎ Sticking to the goal to please God instead of getting sidetracked in too much information.

◎ Tuning out doomsayers and tuning in on God's hope found in His Word.

What **Doesn't** Matter...

◎ What the talking heads are predicting. No one knows the future except God.

◎ What happened last week or last year. You can let go of the past through your hope for eternal joys.

◎ What you wish would happen. It's better to pray and be committed to your given duties than to wish your life away waiting for something that may never happen.

◎ What you give up to be faithful to God's plan. You give up your control to Someone who is so much greater.

◎ What matters most to nonbelievers. Your hope is in the Creator of the universe, not in earthly attainments or success.

Focus Points...

Don't brag about tomorrow, since you don't know what the day will bring.
PROVERBS 27:1 NLT

The world and everything in it that people desire is passing away; but those who do the will of God live forever.
1 JOHN 2:17 GNT

My son, do not forget my teachings, and keep my commands in mind, because they will bring you long life, good years, and peace.
PROVERBS 3:1–2 GOD'S WORD

Do not let your heart envy sinners, but always be zealous for the fear of the LORD. There is surely a future hope for you, and your hope will not be cut off.
PROVERBS 23:17–18 NIV

what really counts

There are always uncertainties ahead, but there is always one certainty—God's will is good.

VERNON PATERSON

I was regretting the past and fearing the future. Suddenly God was speaking:"My name is I am ... My name is not I was ... My name is not I will be. When you live in this moment, it is not hard. I am here. My name is I AM."

HELEN MELLINCOST

The Future
Long-Term Investments

Surely I know the plans I have for you, says
the LORD, plans for your welfare and not for
harm, to give you a future with hope.
                                    JEREMIAH 29:11 NRSV

what really counts

When you're making plans for your future, one area in
which you want to have complete security is your finances.
Maybe you have a business background, and all of this comes
naturally to you. Or you've at least read a few books on the
topic or sought out expert opinion. Any skilled financial
adviser will tell you the best way to weather changes in the
rough-and-tumble marketplace is to diversify your portfolio.
Put some of your assets in high-risk, high-return investments
to try and reap big profits. Then to play it safe, also invest in
some lower risk, lower return markets.

In the same way that you save now to reap benefits later,
you make choices every day to endure a little temporary discomfort in the hopes of reaching a long-term goal. Maybe
you choose that bowl of fruit for dessert and pass up the
enticing, but waist-thickening, slice of cheesecake. Perhaps
you'd rather cruise straight home from work and relax, but

instead, you stop off for another sweaty workout at the gym in the hopes that your heart will keep pumping a few more years.

Besides finances and health, your spiritual portfolio needs attention as well. Are you investing in your prayer life and biblical wisdom? If you're a parent, you may not be seeing much fruit from your early years of investing in your children's scriptural knowledge. Your toddlers may wiggle and poke each other while you read them Bible stories, but your hope is that one day they'll have a deep love for God's Word. Parenting expert Fern Nichols says, "Prayer is the greatest gift you can give your children—and the greatest "work" you can do . . . If you're not praying for your children, who is?"

The expert on long-term planning is of course God, since He already knows what will happen in your future. Jesus makes it very clear when He says, "Where your treasure is, there your heart will be also" (Matthew 6:21 NASB). Don't be like the rich man who kept wanting to build more barns to store his earthly treasures. Jesus said He was a fool who lost his life that very night. "This is how it will be for those who store up things for themselves and are not rich toward God" (Luke 12:21 NCV). If you make it your goal to be rich toward God, you'll be wealthy in that which matters most.

The Future
Long-Term Investments

What Matters Most...

- Investing in long-term spiritual growth.

- Trusting God that you'll reap benefits that are impossible to see now.

- Enduring a little discomfort now to reach your long-term goals.

- Being rich toward God and His wisdom found in Scripture.

- Making sure the treasures of your heart are the same things that God values.

What **Doesn't** Matter...

- Worrying that you aren't seeing any returns yet in your long-term investing.

- Comparing your assets to others who may have different long-term goals.

- Feeling like you're losing earthly pleasures in order to gain heavenly ones.

- Listening to what nonbelievers say you should value as most important.

- Wondering if you're wasting your time when you're spending it on your spiritual portfolio.

Focus Points...

Be on your guard against all kinds of greed; a man's life does not consist in the abundance of his possessions.
LUKE 12:15 NIV

Keep your lives free from the love of money, and be content with what you have; for he has said, "I will never leave you or forsake you."
HEBREWS 13:5 NRSV

I am confident of this very thing, that He who began a good work in you will perfect it until the day of Christ Jesus.
PHILIPPIANS 1:6 NASB

From everyone who has been given much, much will be demanded. And from the one trusted with much, much more will be expected.
LUKE 12:48 NCV

what really counts

Where there is hope, there is optimism. There is assurance that God has not run out of options yet, and neither have we.

DEAN MERRILL

I am well aware of the toil and blood and treasure that it will cost us ...Yet through all the gloom I can see rays of ravishing light and glory. I can see that the end is worth more than all the means.

JOHN ADAMS

What Matters Most to Me About
The Future

It's important to trust God with your future, but it's also a good idea to put in writing the general and the specific goals you'd like to accomplish as a Christian man seeking God's plan for your life. Take a few minutes to reflect on your thoughts about your future.

◎ *Read Romans 5:3–5. Why does Paul say that you should rejoice in your sufferings? What does suffering produce? What is the ultimate goal of hope?*

_____

_____

_____

_____

_____

_____

_____

_____

_____

◎ *What are some specific dreams you have for your future? Do you think God is pleased with your goals?*

_____

_____

_____

_____

_____

_____

_____

what
really
counts

◎ *How will you go about reaching your goals? Are you investing your time and energy into those things that matter most for the long term?*

_____

_____

_____

_____

_____

_____

_____

_____

_____

_____

◎ *List three areas you would like to entrust to God. Take a minute to pray that He will give you peace about giving up your control over these three areas.*

_____

_____

_____

_____

_____

_____

_____

_____

_____

_____

Now is the time to realize that God is the source of our hope and give it all to him. If he can change the heart of a crusty rebel like me, no doubt he can change you and those you love.

KEN DAVIS

WORSHIP

An Introduction

> O magnify the LORD with me, and let us exalt his name together.
>
> PSALM 34:3 NRSV

what really counts

Conference calls. Home maintenance. Business travel. Little League games. Office politics. Modern life pulls you in a hundred different directions every day. The tyranny of the urgent can make it hard to zero in on what matters most.

Worship says, "Forget about all that. Be right here. Right now." Worship is about sitting in the presence of God—experiencing His character, honoring His holiness, delighting in His love. To worship God is to know what the Psalmist knew: "In Your presence is fullness of joy" (Psalm 16:11 NASB). You find more than fleeting happiness in God's presence: You find fullness, you find solidity. Worship is what God put you here for. This is solid joy. Life stretches you thin; worship fattens your soul. Life numbs you; worship brings the feeling back. Life dehumanizes you; worship restores your humanity.

The Bible is clear: Everybody worships something. When you worship, you become like the person or thing you have chosen to worship. When you worship the true God, you become more godly. To practice the presence of God is to rehearse for eternity, when "we will be like Him, because we will see Him just as He is" (1 John 3:2 NASB). The worship of God Almighty transforms you. To experience that kind of love and power—to let it do its work on you—is to move beyond mere human virtue and be conformed to the very image of Christ. This is what you were made for.

> The more a man bows his knee before God, the straighter he stands before men.
>
> AUTHOR UNKNOWN

Worship
God's Worth . . . and Yours

My soul is satisfied as with a rich feast, and my mouth praises you with joyful lips.

PSALM 63:5 NRSV

what really counts

"Your net worth." It's a troubling phrase, isn't it? It makes it sound as if your value as a human being could be reduced to a simple formula: Your assets minus your debts equal your worth. The idea of worth is at the center of worship—not your worth, but God's worth. To worship is to celebrate God's "worth-ship." That celebration is both the starting point and end result of the act of worship. When you get a glimpse of God's worthiness, you fall down and worship; when you fall down and worship, you get a better view of God's worthiness.

To dwell on God's worth is to exult in the truth that God, the greatest of all treasures, has given Himself to you. "Though He was rich, yet for your sake He became poor, so that you through His poverty might become rich" (2 Corinthians 8:9 NASB). In your head, you already know that God is infinitely rich. When you worship, the fact of God's wealth is brought to bear on your heart. It hits you where you live. You can't be silent any more than you could stifle a whoop if you found out your stock portfolio had doubled in value.

There's no such thing as gloomy worship. Worship shifts your life's center of gravity to the place of your deepest joy. It leaves no room for self-pity or self-absorption, but opens you up to the richness that surrounds you. That transforms your life. Are you looking to increase your net worth? Dwell on the worth of God. There's your worthiness, your wealth. As you raise your hands in praise to God, He fills them with more riches than you can get your arms around—joy, significance, eternal life.

In the old Saturday morning cartoons, somebody is always finding a huge pile of money—striking gold, or finding a genie's cave, or inheriting a fortune. Every time, it seems, the newly rich character has the same reaction. He runs in circles shouting, "I'm rich! I'm rich!" He dives into the pile of gold as if into a swimming pool. He splashes around, throwing coins and jewels into the air, and laughing and hooting hysterically. Worship should be a little like that: exuberant celebration, giddy astonishment at the inexplicable, undeserved riches that God has bestowed on you. You're rich! You're rich! You're rich!

Worship
God's Worth . . . and Yours

What Matters Most...

◎ The joy you experience from being in God's presence. He is the greatest of all treasures.

◎ God's joy in being present with you.

◎ The overwhelming reality of God's love for you. He gives you joy, significance, and eternal life.

◎ God's willingness to give Himself freely to you when you worship.

◎ Your staggering spiritual wealth.

What Doesn't Matter...

◎ Financial worth. Your real riches are in heaven.

◎ Feelings of unworthiness. God's worthiness, not yours, is the central fact of worship.

◎ Day-to-day concerns. Nothing is more important than being in God's presence.

◎ Self-pity. Worship shifts your focus to what you have in God, and away from what you lack.

◎ Self-doubt. God's sufficiency overwhelms your insufficiency.

Focus Points...

Give unto the LORD the glory due to His name; worship the LORD in the beauty of holiness.
PSALM 29:2 NKJV

Now I can rest again, for the LORD has been so good to me.
PSALM 116:7 NLT

Let us come before His presence with thanksgiving, let us shout joyfully to Him with psalms.
PSALM 95:2 NASB

I am always aware of the LORD 's presence; he is near, and nothing can shake me.
PSALM 16:8 GNT

what
really
counts

It would be very difficult to draw a line between holy wonder and *real worship*; for when the soul is overwhelmed with the majesty of God's glory, though it may not express itself in song, or even utter its voice with bowed head in humble prayer, yet it silently adores.

CHARLES H. SPURGEON

Worship is to feel in your heart and express in some appropriate manner a humbling but delightful sense of admiring awe and astonished wonder and overpowering love in the presence of that most ancient Mystery, that Majesty which philosophers call the First Cause, but which we call Our Father Which Are in Heaven.

A. W. TOZER

Worship
Surprising Joy

He put a new song in my mouth, a song of praise to our God; many will see and fear and will trust in the Lord.

PSALM 40:3 NASB

In one of the great old hymns, William Cowper speaks of the divine joy that sneaks up when you least expect it: "Sometimes a light surprises the Christian as he sings. It is the Lord, who rises with healing in His wings. When comforts are declining, he gives the soul again A season of clear shining to cheer it after rain." Those weren't empty words for Cowper. This was a man who suffered bouts of severe, even debilitating depression throughout his life. Yet he continued to worship God through that, and time and time again God astonished him with a shaft of light that cut through his black despair.

The remarkable thing about that scene isn't just that God intervened and brought joy where there had been despair and sorrow. Just as remarkable is the fact that Cowper, in the midst of depression, had the good sense to sing a song of praise. Depressed people don't feel like worshiping. You can picture Cowper mouthing his way through a hymn, just going through the motions, but even then, God shone through.

There's a wrong way to "go through the motions" of worship. God condemns the hypocrisy of those who pay Him lip service with no desire to serve Him, but there's also a right kind of "going through the motions." It's when you say, "God, my heart's not in this, but I want my heart to be in it. You call me to worship, so here goes." You worship God the best you can and trust God to meet you there. God honors that kind of obedience and rewards it.

You can't afford to worship only when you feel like it. In fact, the times you least feel like worshiping are the very times you need the transforming experience of worship the most. Sure, in the best-case scenario, worship rises spontaneously out of your joy in Christ. What a blessing when that's your experience! But sometimes it works the other way around. The act of worship gives rise to joy. Sometimes all you have to bring to God is doubt, fear, sin, sadness. Bring those things to God too, and worship the best you can. Sing a song of praise. Meditate on the mind-boggling truth that the Maker of the universe loves you as an individual. Pray a prayer, even if you don't feel like praying. Sometimes God's light surprises you.

Worship
Surprising Joy

What Matters Most...

◎ Your expectation to meet God in the act of worship.

◎ Your willingness to bring your whole self—including your doubts and sins—before God in worship.

◎ God's willingness to meet you where you are.

◎ God's power to bring joy out of sadness, light out of darkness.

◎ A heart of obedience. Worship the best you can. God honors obedience and rewards it.

What **Doesn't** Matter...

◎ Your emotional state. Worship gives you a new perspective on things.

◎ Your doubts about the future. Worship puts you in touch with the God who holds the future.

◎ Your sin. Worship is a first step in repentance.

◎ Your coldness to the things of God. Worship warms your heart.

◎ Your inability to comprehend the ways of God. You know enough to bow down to Him.

Focus Points...

Oh, worship the LORD in the beauty of holiness! Tremble before Him, all the earth.
PSALM 96:9 NKJV

You will have songs as in the night when you keep the festival, and gladness of heart as when one marches to the sound of the flute, to go to the mountain of the LORD, to the Rock of Israel.
ISAIAH 30:29 NASB

Because of your great love I can come into your house; I can worship in your holy Temple and bow down to you in reverence.
PSALM 5:7 GNT

what really counts

The Scotch catechism says that man's chief end is "to glorify God and enjoy Him forever." But we shall then [in Heaven] know that they are the same thing. Fully to enjoy is to glorify. In commanding us to glorify Him, God is commanding us to enjoy Him.

C. S. LEWIS

God hates hypocrisy. He doesn't want showmanship or pretense or phoniness in worship. He wants your honest, real love. We can worship God imperfectly, but we cannot worship him insincerely.

RICK WARREN

What Matters Most to Me About
Worship

Worship is about honoring God's worth-ship and finding your own worth in the process. It's about transcending the world you can see and catching a spiritual glimpse of the world you were made for. Isn't that worth your time and energy?

◎ *Remember some times in the past when you have experienced "real" worship. What were those experiences like?*

_____

_____

_____

_____

_____

_____

_____

_____

what
really
counts

◎ *Can you identify barriers that keep you from worshiping "in spirit and in truth"? How can you address them?*

_____

_____

_____

_____

_____

_____

_____

◉ *What aspects of worship have the most profound effect on you?*

_____

_____

_____

_____

_____

_____

_____

_____

_____

◉ *Where do you feel most comfortable worshiping?*

_____

_____

_____

_____

_____

_____

_____

_____

_____

I appeal to you therefore, brothers and sisters,
by the mercies of God, to present your bodies
as a living sacrifice, holy and acceptable to God,
which is your spiritual worship.

Romans 12:1 NRSV

WORSHIP

THE CHURCH

An Introduction

> Now you Gentiles are ... citizens along with all of God's holy people. You are members of God's family.
>
> EPHESIANS 2:19 NLT

what really counts

In 1 Corinthians 12, the apostle Paul described the Church as a body with Christ as its head. It's a great image of unity in diversity. Every body part is different in form and function, and yet each part has vital role to play. The eye is one of the more high-profile and glamorous of the body parts, but what would happen if the whole body were an eye? Sure, it would see great, but how would it hear? How would it get the oxygen it needs without lungs, heart, and blood vessels? The body depends on each of its members, however small or undignified it seems to be. In the same way, the Church depends on each of its members to bring his or her particular gifts to the larger work.

Each member depends on the body. What would happen, Paul asked, if the foot got jealous of the hand and, deciding it had no place in the body, struck out on its own? A foot obviously doesn't have what it takes to make it on its own. In the same way, you need the body of believers. Cut off from the body, it wouldn't be long before you shriveled spiritually.

It's no wonder then, that the writer of Hebrews urges Christians not to neglect the gathering together of the body of believers. The body needs each of its members, and no member can make it apart from the body. This is not a casual thing.

> There are many things which a person can do alone, but being a Christian is not one of them ... The personal relationship to Christ can only be realized when one has "come to himself" as a member of His Body, the Christian fellowship.
>
> WILLIAM T. HAM

The Church
God's Trophy Case

Listen, dear friends. Isn't it clear by now that God operates quite differently? He chose the world's down-and-out as the kingdom's first citizens, with full rights and privileges. This kingdom is promised to anyone who loves God.

JAMES 2:5 MSG

what really counts

When Gideon looked out across the battle camp, his force wasn't exactly overwhelming. Thirty thousand men, mostly shepherds, farmers and craftsmen. Now they were supposed to be an army. The Midianites—battle-hardened, cruel, and so numerous as to be uncountable—were encamped just to the north of Gideon's ragtag army. It seemed obvious: Gideon needed more soldiers. But God had a different plan. At God's command, Gideon reduced his force to ten thousand men, then to three hundred. Those three hundred men were all God needed to destroy the Midianite invaders.

God is something of a show-off. He delights in showing forth His power, His holiness, His grace. It's how He draws people to Himself, causes them to trust in Him and not in their own power. That's what the Gideon story is all about. If thirty thousand Israelites had defeated the Midianite horde, they might have congratulated themselves on their military prowess. Perhaps even ten thousand men would have, but when three hundred men defeat one of the world's great armies, there's no question that it's God who is at work.

That's the story of the Church throughout the ages. God takes ordinary people, flawed people, obscure people, and forms them into the body of Christ, showing the world what it looks like when lives are transformed by the love of God. Consider Paul's words to the church at Corinth: "You see your calling, brethren, that not many wise according to the flesh, not many mighty, not many noble, are called. But God has chosen the foolish things of the world to put to shame the wise . . . and the things which are not, to bring to nothing the things that are, that no flesh should glory in His presence" (1 Corinthians 1:26–29 NKJV). God's doesn't need superstars or geniuses or power brokers to do His work in the world.

God has many ways of showing His glory in the world and drawing people to trust in Him. One of the most important is His Church. Sometimes it can be frustrating to look around your local church and see what imperfect people inhabit it. You might wonder how a bunch of ordinary, flawed people are supposed to show forth God's glory. But every changed life—however imperfect it may be—is an accomplishment of God's mercy and grace. Every believer is a trophy of God's grace. The Church is God's trophy case.

The Church
God's Trophy Case

What Matters Most...

◎ God's glory. He's determined to show it to a watching world.

◎ God's habit of showing His strength through weakness. You don't have to be perfect to be used of God.

◎ Your talents and gifts. God wants to use them.

◎ Your willingness to serve. Your talents aren't just for your benefit.

◎ The worldwide Church. You're part of something larger than your local church.

What Doesn't Matter...

◎ The failures of particular church leaders. They're human too; but the Church is of God.

◎ The culture's obliviousness to the Church. It doesn't matter what the world sees or doesn't see; when Christ sees the Church, He sees His bride.

◎ Your feelings of smallness. Together with the rest of the Church, you're huge.

◎ Your shortcomings. God is looking for a willing heart, not a perfect track record.

◎ The shortcomings of your fellow church members. God's strength is made perfect in weakness.

Focus Points...

Where is the wise? Where is the scribe? Where is the disputer of this age? Has not God made foolish the wisdom of this world?
1 Corinthians 1:20 NKJV

I am the vine, you are the branches. He who abides in Me, and I in him, bears much fruit; for without Me you can do nothing.
John 15:5 NKJV

You should not stay away from the church meetings, as some are doing, but you should meet together and encourage each other. Do this even more as you see the day coming.
Hebrews 10:25 NCV

what really counts

The church is: a conspiracy of love for a dying world, a spy mission into enemy-occupied territory ruled by the powers of evil; a prophet from God with the greatest news the world has ever heard, the most life-changing and most revolutionary institution that has existed on earth.

Peter Kreeft

It does not take a perfect church to introduce a man to the perfect Christ.

Richard Woodsome

153

The Church
The Stones of God's Dwelling

> We are his house, built on the foundation
> of the apostles and the prophets. And the
> cornerstone is Christ Jesus himself
>
> EPHESIANS 2:20 NLT

There are many possible building materials for a church structure. The quarried stone of the great cathedrals, the white clapboard of a little country church, the aluminum siding of many contemporary churches. The Bible specifies the best—indeed, the only—building material for the 'capital-C' Church: believers. "Present yourselves as building stones for the construction of a sanctuary vibrant with life, in which you'll serve as holy priests offering Christ-approved lives up to God" (1 Peter 2:5 MSG). The dwelling place of God on earth is within the people who make up the Church. No building has ever been God's dwelling place—not the incredibly beautiful cathedrals of Europe, not even the Temple of Old Testament Jerusalem. People like you, held together by the mortar of God's love, make up the house of God.

It was Peter who wrote those words about living stones. The name *Peter*, you may remember, means "stone" or "rock."

When Jesus gave him that name, He said, "On this rock I will build my church, and the power of death will not be able to defeat it" (Matthew 16:18 NCV). So Peter knew a thing or two about being a living stone. Yet even Peter, the Rock, acknowledges that the true Cornerstone of the Church is Christ (see 1 Peter 2). Christ the Cornerstone squares up the spiritual masonry of the Church, gives it stability and cohesion.

You may be a little rough around the edges. You won't be perfectly square as long as you live in your human body. But if you are in Christ, you are a stone in an edifice that puts even the most ornate church building to shame. The Church has stood for over two thousand years, and every day it grows a little larger. Every time a stone is added, it shows forth God's glory in some new way. It stretches across the world, across cultures, across languages. No scandal, no persecution, not even apathy can destroy the Church that God has built stone by stone. God shows the world what he is like by building His people into a Church.

The Church is people, not buildings. Together they form a dwelling where God can live and do His work on earth. If you are in Christ, you are joined with Him, the Cornerstone. You are part of something huge and hugely important. You have no higher calling.

The Church
The Stones of God's Dwelling

What Matters Most...

◉ Christ, the Cornerstone. Without the Cornerstone, the building could not stand.

◉ Your connection with other believers. Together you are built into something beautiful.

◉ The presence of God. Where two are three are gathered in His name, He is there.

◉ Strength in numbers. A single strand is easily broken, but a many-stranded cable is not.

◉ The grand sweep of Church history. You have a part to play in something as big as that.

What **Doesn't** Matter...

◉ The kind of building you worship in. God calls you to worship Him in spirit and in truth.

◉ Your "rugged individualism." You need other believers; you need to be part of something larger than yourself.

◉ Your social status. The Church is made up of all sorts of people.

◉ The imperfections of your fellow Church members. God is still working on them, too.

◉ The difficulties faced by the Church. Not even the gates of hell will prevail against it.

Focus Points...

In him you too are being built together to become a dwelling in which God lives by his Spirit.
EPHESIANS 2:22 NIV

Speaking the truth with love, we will grow up in every way into Christ, who is the head.
EPHESIANS 4:15 NCV

No other foundation can anyone lay than that which is laid, which is Jesus Christ.
1 CORINTHIANS 3:11 NKJV

Where two or three are gathered in my name, I am there among them.
MATTHEW 18:20 NRSV

what really counts

Every Christian community must realize that not only do the weak need the strong, but also that the strong cannot exist without the weak. The elimination of the weak is the death of the fellowship.

DIETRICH BONHOEFFER

Christians in community must again show the world, not merely family values, but the bond of the love of Christ ... Only as the church binds together those whom selfishness and hate have cut apart will its message be heard and its ministry of hope to the friendless be received.

EDMUND CLOWNEY

What Matters Most to Me About
The Church

When you enter the family of God through your faith in Jesus, you become part of the body of Christ. He is the head, and you are part of the body that will build Him up and bring Him glory. Take a few minutes to think about your role in the church.

◎ *Have you ever taken a survey of your spiritual gifts? Talk to someone in your church or find a book that contains a test. What do you think your gifts are?*

_____

_____

_____

_____

_____

_____

_____

_____

_____

◎ *How do you think God can use you in the church to bring Him glory and to serve others?*

_____

_____

_____

_____

_____

_____

_____

○ Do you think you have the kind of faith that will take you from being ordinary to extraordinary? What helps or hinders you in your faith?

_____

_____

_____

_____

_____

_____

_____

_____

_____

_____

○ Describe one of your favorite times of fellowship that has taken place within God's family.

_____

_____

_____

_____

_____

_____

_____

_____

_____

_____

I go to church, not because of any legalistic or moralistic reasons, but because I am a hungry sheep who needs to be fed; and for the same reason that I wear a wedding ring: a public witness of a private commitment.

MADELEINE L'ENGLE

WISDOM

An Introduction

> Wisdom begins with respect for the LORD; those who obey his orders have good understanding. He should be praised forever.
>
> PSALM 111:10 NCV

what really counts

A verse in Proverbs reveals a lot about the difference between wisdom and foolishness: "A fool does not delight in understanding, but only in revealing his own mind" (Proverbs 18:2 NASB). A wise man, by contrast, does delight in understanding. It's hard work to gain understanding. One of the obvious benefits of that hard work is the fact that people are impressed by your knowledge. It's gratifying when people want to hear you speak your mind. A fool tries to skip over the hard work and jump straight to the benefit. He speaks his mind in the vain hope that people will be impressed with him.

Wisdom is just another word for "delayed gratification." A wise man knows that the good life is the reward of the hard work that goes into building a life of substance. A fool will always try to short-circuit the process and jump to the reward, but it never works. He gets the Jaguar, perhaps, but the car payments leave him with no money to buy gas for it.

Everything a fool hopes to avoid, he eventually runs smack into. "The slack hand will be put to forced labor" (Proverbs 12:24 NASB). The big spender ends up in bankruptcy court. Conversely, a wise man always finds more than he looks for. "He who pursues right-eousness and loyalty finds life, righteousness and honor" (Proverbs 21:21 NASB). The wise man looks to do the right thing. He's rewarded with honor on top of the righteousness he sought. That's not a bad deal.

We are ensnared by the wisdom of the serpent; we are set free by the foolishness of God.

SAINT AUGUSTINE

Wisdom
Choosing Happiness

> We set our eyes not on what we see but on what we cannot see. What we see will last only a short time, but what we cannot see will last forever.
>
> 2 CORINTHIANS 4:18 NCV

what really counts

You have probably received hundreds, maybe even thousands of credit card offers in your lifetime. A credit card is a true test of wisdom. It promises freedom and security, but if you're not wise, that freedom begins to feel a lot like slavery after the low introductory APR expires. You realize that you haven't bought security; you've sold it, and way too cheaply. Every credit card offer has the same promise, whether implied or explicit: Whatever it is that you want, you can have it right now. You don't have to wait for it. You don't have to work for it. The problem, of course, is that you do have to work for it. You may still be working for it long after it's broken or out of style—long after you have the hankering for your next big purchase on your next credit card.

Wisdom, when you boil it down, is the art of getting what you want the most and rejecting all other offers. If that sounds like an overly selfish definition, consider God's promise: "Delight yourself also in the LORD, and He shall give you the desires of your heart" (Psalm 37:4 NKJV). What do you want the most? After you've answered that question, answer another: If you were to get what you say you want the most, what need do you think that would fulfill? Because that's what you really want. If you want a Harley-Davidson because you think it will make you feel free, it's freedom you really want, not a motorcycle.

The point is, every choice you make is an attempt to pursue happiness, but it's easy to get off track. You live in a consumer culture where marketers blur the distinction between legitimate desires—to be happy, to be loved, to feel secure, to feel manly—and products that supposedly fulfill those desires. The problem isn't just consumer products. The world offers up millions of substitutes and shortcuts to the life you want.

How do you get what you want? The first step, perhaps, is to realize that there aren't really any shortcuts. If you want to feel manly, act like a man. If you want friendship, be a friend. Love your wife, fulfill your responsibilities, take care of those who are weaker than you. The happiness you seek is the reward of a life well-lived. That's real wisdom.

Wisdom
Choosing Happiness

What Matters Most...

◎ Valuing things rightly. Wise people know what matters most.

◎ Believing God. Wisdom takes faith in God's promises.

◎ Foresight. Wise people can picture the consequences of their actions.

◎ Insight. Wise people don't just know; they understand.

◎ Hindsight. Wise people learn from the past.

What **Doesn't** Matter...

◎ Shortcuts. There aren't any shortcuts to wisdom or happiness; there is only the life well-lived.

◎ False offers of happiness that constantly demands your attention. Deeper happiness is usually quiet, but it's not hard to find.

◎ The desire to have it all right now. It takes time to get what you really want—what really matters.

◎ The lure of easy happiness. Don't sell your future for a short-term thrill.

◎ Your natural foolishness. God gives wisdom to those who ask.

Focus Points...

You have given him his heart's desire, and have not with-
held the request of his lips.
PSALM 21:2 NKJV

It is senseless to pay tuition to educate a fool who has no
heart for wisdom.
PROVERBS 17:16 NLT

Oh, the depth of the riches both of the wisdom and knowledge of God! How unsearchable are His judgments and His
ways past finding out!
ROMANS 11:33 NKJV

In [Christ] all the treasures of wisdom and knowledge are
safely kept.
COLOSSIANS 2:3 NCV

**what
really
counts**

Wisdom is the power to see and the inclination to choose
the best and highest goal, together with the surest means
of attaining it.

J. I. PACKER

God guides us first through his Word, then through our
heartfelt desires, then the wise counsel of others, and then
our circumstances. At that point we must rely on our own
sound judgment . . . God gave each of us a brain, and he
expects us to put it to good use.

BRUCE K. WALTKE

Wisdom
There for the Asking

> Happy is the person who finds wisdom,
> the one who gets understanding.
> PROVERBS 3:13 NCV

what really counts

Imagine you're sitting in an open bank vault. Bundles of bills, bags of coins, bars of gold bullion are piled all around you. Now imagine the bank president invites you to take as much as you like. If you leave empty-handed, whose fault is that? In the same way, all the riches of godly wisdom are available for you—there for the asking. "If any of you lacks wisdom, let him ask of God, who gives to all liberally and without reproach, and it will be given to him" (James 1:5 NKJV). Neglecting to ask for wisdom is like walking out of that bank vault with empty pockets. If you lack the wisdom that God offers freely, whose fault is that?

Consider what people are willing to pay for knowledge. College and graduate school tuition, incredibly high already, outpace inflation year after year. Business consultants of various kinds collect astronomical fees to share their knowledge in specialized fields, but knowledge doesn't do a lot of good (and has the potential to do much harm) without the wisdom to know what to do with it. Wisdom has more to do with judgment than with knowledge of the facts. Knowledge tells you what the facts are. Wisdom tells you which facts matter, and how those facts contribute to a life well lived. Wisdom doesn't have to be all that expensive.

That's not to say that wisdom comes easily. You don't just pray for wisdom, then find yourself mysteriously and suddenly wise, as if a genie had clapped his hands. Wisdom does take time. It takes a long desire in the same direction. It takes a commitment to God's Word and to prayer. But if wisdom is what you really want, you'll get it. Because the very desire for wisdom is in itself a kind of wisdom. It's a desire that matches up with God's desire for your life. He wouldn't withhold it from you any more than a parent would withhold a carrot from a child who wanted to increase her intake of vitamins.

God invites you to be as rich as you want to be. "Wisdom is better than rubies, and all the things one may desire cannot be compared with her" (Proverbs 8:11 NKJV). The most valuable treasure of all is yours for the asking. How rich do you want to be?

Wisdom
There for the Asking

What Matters Most...

- Making the request. Wisdom is yours for the asking.

- Searching the Scriptures. Wisdom doesn't come all at once. God applies it to your heart and mind as you seek it in His Word.

- Truly wanting wisdom. You can be as wise as you want to be.

- God's supply. He has more than enough wisdom to give.

- God's generosity. He delights to give wisdom to those who ask.

What **Doesn't** Matter...

- Age. You don't have to be an old man to be wise.

- Lack of experience. Experience is a good teacher, but it isn't the only teacher.

- Position. You don't have to hold an important position to be wise.

- Your mistakes. God uses your mistakes to grow you in wisdom.

- Education. Wisdom is about making good choices, not having a head full of facts.

Focus Points...

Every good gift and every perfect gift is from above, and comes down from the Father of lights, with whom there is no variation or shadow of turning.
JAMES 1:17 NKJV

Jesus has the power of God, by which he has given us everything we need to live and to serve God. We have these things because we know him. Jesus called us by his glory and goodness.
2 PETER 1:3 NCV

Scripture says, "I will destroy the wisdom of the wise. I will reject the intelligence of intelligent people."
1 CORINTHIANS 1:19 GOD'S WORD

With her right hand wisdom offers you a long life, and with her left hand she gives you riches and honor. Wisdom will make your life pleasant and will bring you peace.
PROVERBS 3:16–17 NCV

what really counts

Never mistake knowledge for wisdom. One helps you make a living; the other helps you make a life.

SANDRA CAREY

A wise man can see more from the bottom of a well than a fool can from a mountain top.

PROVERB

What Matters Most to Me About
Wisdom

Wisdom is yours for the asking. But it doesn't come all at once; nor does it come without some effort on your part. Spend some time reflecting on the importance of wisdom in your life.

◎ *Wisdom is about shaping your everyday life around what is truly valuable. If someone were to follow you around and observe your every action for a week, what would they say you value?*

_____

_____

_____

_____

_____

_____

_____

_____

◎ *What mistakes have you made that have added to your store of wisdom? How about the mistakes of others?*

_____

_____

_____

_____

_____

_____

_____

_____

what really counts

You face decisions that will require lots of wisdom. Write a prayer asking God for the wisdom you need.

_____

_____

_____

_____

_____

_____

_____

_____

_____

_____

Think of a person whose wisdom you admire. How is he different from other people you know?

_____

_____

_____

_____

_____

_____

_____

_____

_____

_____

Knowledge is proud that he has learned so much; wisdom is humble that he knows no more.

WILLIAM COWPER

WISDOM

PURPOSE

An Introduction

> I do not run without a goal. I fight like a boxer who is hitting something—not just the air.
>
> 1 CORINTHIANS 9:26 NCV

what really counts

There's a legend that Alexander the Great cried when he realized he had no more worlds to conquer. The story is probably untrue, but nevertheless it makes an interesting comment on one man's sense of purpose. The world could offer no grander scope of purpose than Alexander's. He wanted it all, and he got it. Yet it still wasn't enough.

If your sense of purpose isn't centered on a relationship with God, you won't feel that your purpose is worthy of you. Indeed, if your ambitions don't go beyond the things of earth, they can't possibly be worthy of you. You weren't made for this earth. That's why the whole world wasn't big enough to satisfy Alexander's ambition. It isn't big enough to satisfy yours either.

The apostle Paul said he had only one ambition: to be pleasing to God (see 2 Corinthians 5:9). That ambition captivated him. It caused him to endure shipwrecks, snakebite, beatings, scourging, imprisonment. Yet none of those things ever took away his joy. None of that suffering made him weep with frustration the way Alexander's incredible success made him weep. "I press on," wrote Paul, "so that I may lay hold of that for which also I was laid hold of by Christ Jesus" (Philippians 3:12 NASB). What an amazing way to put it. Paul's striving was motivated by a certainty of purpose: He was only grabbing hold of what Christ had already grabbed on his behalf. Is your life marked by that kind of purpose?

> Everyone who breathes, high and low, educated and ignorant, young and old, man and woman, has a mission, has a work. We are not sent into this world for nothing.
>
> JOHN HENRY NEWMAN

Purpose
Led, Not Driven

Why do you spend money for what is not bread, and your wages for what does not satisfy? Listen carefully to Me, and eat what is good, and let your soul delight itself in abundance.

ISAIAH 55:2 NKJV

It's usually said in an admiring voice: "Man, is that guy driven." Driven to succeed. Driven to win. Driven to be the best. It's the ultimate description of the striver, the go-getter who is not content to be passive or to take no for an answer. Isn't it ironic, then, that, grammatically speaking, the phrase is a passive construction? It's not, "That man is driving to succeed." It's "That man is driven." In other words, something is driving him. You picture him with a lash at his back, laboring to keep one step ahead of the taskmaster.

what really counts

The drive to succeed doesn't seem so admirable when you think of it in those terms. Yet you know people—perhaps you're one of them—for whom success is a hard master, driving them to exhaustion, demanding that anyone in its service give up the things that matter most. Answering the drive to succeed is not the same thing as having a purpose for your life. Staying busy isn't the same thing as being diligent. A full schedule isn't the same thing as a full life.

174

Throughout Scripture you're called to be diligent in your work and diligent in the work of God's kingdom, but you are never called to work yourself to a frazzle. There's little joy in work when you're striving to prove yourself. "Come to Me, all you who labor and are heavy laden," said Jesus, "and I will give you rest. Take My yoke upon you and learn from Me . . . for My yoke is easy and My burden is light" (Matthew 11:28–30 NKJV). Elsewhere He describes Himself as a Good Shepherd, gently leading His sheep. Christ is no slave driver, but neither does He leave you to wander aimlessly or self-indulgently. He has a path for your life, and He leads you in the path.

As long as you're looking for purpose and significance in the things of earth, the natural progression is to be more and more driven, or else just to give up and settle into a vague purposelessness. But if you find your purpose in the things of heaven—if you're walking in the path that God has for your life—you'll find that your life is characterized by peace, not the drive to succeed or to prove yourself. You'll find that you're led by a gentle master, not a slave driver.

Purpose
Led, Not Driven

What Matters Most...

◎ Walking the path God has for you. He will lead you in it. He will not let you wander aimlessly.

◎ Obeying God. He has important work for you to do.

◎ Resting in God. He's the Good Shepherd. You are never called to work yourself to a frazzle.

◎ Seeing God in the ordinary. He has a purpose for your whole life.

◎ Aligning your will with God's. His plan is better than yours.

What Doesn't Matter...

◎ Knowing God's whole purpose for your life. You're walking by faith, not by sight.

◎ Earthly success. God doesn't take His definition of success from the world's dictionary.

◎ Being driven. Let yourself be led instead.

◎ A full schedule. You have to leave some time for quietness if you want to stay attuned to God's purposes for you.

◎ Self-direction. God will direct your steps if you trust in Him.

Focus Points...

To me, to live is Christ, and to die is gain.
PHILIPPIANS 1:21 NKJV

My ego is no longer central. It is no longer important that I appear righteous before you or have your good opinion, and I am no longer driven to impress God. Christ lives in me. The life you see me living is not "mine," but it is lived by faith in the Son of God, who loved me and gave himself for me.
GALATIANS 2:20 MSG

Blessed is the man who trusts me, GOD, the woman who sticks with GOD. They're like trees replanted in Eden, putting down roots near the rivers—never a worry through the hottest of summers, never dropping a leaf.
JEREMIAH 17:7–8 MSG

GOD made everything with a place and purpose.
PROVERBS 16:4 MSG

what really counts

The chief end of man is to glorify God and enjoy him forever.

WESTMINSTER SHORTER CATECHISM

Knowing that we are fulfilling God's purpose is the only thing that really gives rest to the restless human heart.

CHARLES COLSON

Purpose
Knowing God's Will

Lord, tell me your ways. Show
me how to live.

Psalm 25:4 NCV

**what
really
counts**

When you hike a forest trail, you can't see the end of the
trail, but you can always see enough to get there. You can see
to take your next steps, then your next two steps, until you
eventually arrive at your destination. You might know from
the map that the trailhead is five miles away, but you still have
to take the trail as it comes. That's why you go hiking in the
first place. Otherwise, you'd just sit home and look at the
map.

Seeking the will of God for your life is a little like hiking
that forest trail. You can see God's will for your life, but you
can't see all of it. You can see enough to stay on the trail. You
know from God's Word where the trail eventually leads. What
you don't know is what lies around the next bend.

Theologians make a helpful distinction between God's
providential will, His moral will, and His individual will.
God's providential will is His plan for all of human history.

178

He will defeat Satan, redeem His Church, and usher His people into heaven. Nothing can thwart that plan. This is the big picture, the trail map. God's moral will is about sin and righteousness. It's His will that you love Him with all your heart, soul, mind, and strength, and love your neighbor as yourself. Like His providential will, God's moral will is spelled out in the Bible. By following God's moral will one step at a time, one choice at a time, you keep yourself on the trail. Drift away from it, and you'll soon find yourself lost in the woods. But then there's God's individual will for your life—the specifics of where you should work, whom you should marry, what's going to become of your children. This is what people usually mean when they talk about "seeking the will of God." Yet it's the hardest part of God's will to know.

It's a fact of human existence: You can't see around the next bend. But you can see enough to take the next step. When you get to the next bend, you'll be able to see to take the next step there too. Live by that part of God's will that you do know—stay on the trail—and the more mysterious parts will reveal themselves in their time.

Purpose
Knowing God's Will

What Matters Most...

◉ Praying for guidance. God will show you His purposes one step at a time.

◉ Being patient. You can't know the whole story yet.

◉ Trusting God. He's the one who laid out the path, and His path is perfect.

◉ Staying on the path. One choice at a time, you can keep yourself out of the woods.

◉ Following as much of God's will as you can see. The rest will reveal itself in time.

What **Doesn't** Matter...

◉ Your agenda. It's about God's plan, not yours.

◉ Your abilities. God equips you to do what he's called you to do.

◉ Your timetable. Trust God to give you what you need, when you need it.

◉ Your idea of success. As you seek God, your idea of success will start to look more like His.

◉ Your mistakes. When you realize you've strayed from the path, get back on it.

Focus Points...

Trust in the LORD with all your heart, and lean not on your own understanding; in all your ways acknowledge Him, and He shall direct your paths.
PROVERBS 3:5–6 NKJV

The path of life is level for those who are right with God; LORD, you make the way of life smooth for those people.
ISAIAH 26:7 NCV

Train me, GOD, to walk straight; then I'll follow your true path. Put me together, one heart and mind; then, undivided, I'll worship in joyful fear.
PSALM 86:11 MSG

O LORD, I know the way of man is not in himself; it is not in man who walks to direct his own steps.
JEREMIAH 10:23 NKJV

what really counts

When God is involved, anything can happen ... Be open. Stay that way. God has a beautiful way of bringing good vibrations out of broken chords.

CHARLES SWINDOLL

A saint's life is in the hands of God as a bow and arrow in the hands of an archer. God is aiming at something the saint cannot see; he stretches and strains, and every now and again the saint says, "I cannot stand any more." But God does not heed; he goes on stretching until his purpose is in sight, then he lets fly.

OSWALD CHAMBERS

What Matters Most to Me About
Purpose

God created you with an intense desire to know Him personally, and your main purpose in life is to worship and enjoy Him. What steps can you take to be active in fulfilling His desires for you?

◎ *Seek God in prayer. What major things—burning on your heart right now—would you really like to place before the Lord?*

_____

_____

_____

_____

_____

_____

_____

_____

◎ *Seek God in worship. What are some different ways you can express praise to God today?*

_____

_____

_____

_____

_____

_____

_____

◎ *Seek God in His Word. Read Isaiah 64:8. In what ways do you feel like clay that is being shaped by the Potter?*

_____

_____

_____

_____

_____

_____

_____

_____

_____

◎ *Can you name anyone whom you can see has changed gradually over time to fulfill a more noble purpose? Perhaps it is a friend, a member of your family, or someone famous.*

_____

_____

_____

_____

_____

_____

_____

_____

_____

O God, Thou hast made us for thyself, and ours hearts are restless until they find their rest in Thee.

SAINT AUGUSTINE

PEACE AND HAPPINESS
An Introduction

> The mind set on the flesh is death, but the mind set on the Spirit is life and peace.
>
> ROMANS 8:6 NASB

what really counts

The naturalist John Muir once announced that he was wealthier than the railroad tycoon E. J. Harriman, who at the time was one of the richest men in the world. "I have as much money as I want," Muir explained, "and he doesn't." That comment gets at the heart of what it means to experience peace and happiness. To be content with what you have is the beginning of a happy life.

If you choose to dwell on those things that God has not blessed you with, you can be sure that peace and happiness won't hang around for long. You serve a God who always, always gives you what you need. In the end, He always gives you what you want too, even if it's not obvious on the front end. Still, you can always figure out some way to feel slighted, if that's what you want. Or you can be content and embrace the good life that God has offered you.

Abraham Lincoln once turned down a job applicant, giving only the explanation, "I don't like his face." A cabinet member protested that this was insufficient grounds for not hiring the man. But Lincoln stood his ground, saying, "Every man over forty is responsible for his face." He was right. All day every day you're making choices that play themselves out on your face. You can become more content and happy, or you can become sour and disgruntled. Which face are you presenting to the world?

How completely satisfying to turn from our limitations to a God who has none ... God never hurries. There are no deadlines against which he must work. To know this is to quiet our spirits and relax our nerves.

A. W. TOZER

Peace and Happiness
A Life of Gratitude

> In everything give thanks; for this is the will of God in Christ Jesus for you.
>
> 1 Thessalonians 5:18 NKJV

what really counts

The consummate gesture of gratitude in this culture is probably the thank-you note. The writing of thank-you notes is becoming something of a lost art, especially among men. Yet a heart-felt thank-you note means a lot to the recipient. It lets that person know that their act of generosity did not go unnoticed. It confirms him or her in the belief that kindness is the right way to go.

Almost by definition, thank-you note gratitude is backward-looking and reactive. Somebody does something nice for you, and you react with a thank-you note. That's obviously a good thing. But an even better thing—the gratitude that really changes your life—is a habit of gratitude. Habitual gratitude is really a worldview more than a reaction to individual acts of generosity. It's a mindset that sees every day as a gift from God, and every challenge as an opportunity to see God work in your life. Habitual gratitude doesn't merely look backwards. It looks around too, constantly seeking out something to be thankful for. Habitual gratitude is like static electricity: It floats free, almost like an aura around a person, waiting for an opportunity to zap out and express itself.

Habitual gratitude says, "Neither God nor the universe owes me the good things I experience every day. Those things are blessings." The result is a constant thankfulness. Habitual gratitude says, "I couldn't be what I am today without the goodness of God and the kindness of other people." So even your own accomplishments become occasions more for thanksgiving than for self-congratulation. Habitual gratitude conditions you to accept even the hardships of life with a peaceful spirit and a confidence that the God who has given you so many good gifts will work even your difficulties to your good.

Gratitude is a vital part of a life of peace and happiness. There's more to genuine gratitude than making God or another person feel good for having done you a good turn. Gratitude completes your enjoyment of the blessings you've been given; it allows those blessings to do their work on you. An ungrateful, selfish heart cracks open just enough to snatch at an offered blessing, then closes back on itself. A grateful heart, by contrast, is an open heart, always ready to receive the blessings of God and the generosity of other people. The habit of gratitude is the habit of happiness.

Peace and Happiness
A Life of Gratitude

What Matters Most...

- The blessings in your life. When you acknowledge them, they can enrich your life.

- Abundance. Those who are ready to receive God's blessing in their lives find that He blesses them to overflowing.

- The habit of gratitude. True gratitude is a lifestyle of seeking out the good in your life and getting the most out of it.

- Relationships. A grateful spirit strengthens your relationship both with God and with the people around you.

- Contentment. Gratitude makes you content with what you have.

What Doesn't Matter...

- A grudging thanks. Genuine gratitude comes from the inside out.

- The blessings you haven't been given. Dwelling on what you don't have is a shortcut to misery.

- The myth of the self-made man. You are what you are because God has been good to you and the people in your life have helped you along.

- The seeming randomness with which blessings are distributed. God has a plan, even if you don't understand it.

- The tendency toward selfishness. Gratitude is the great enemy of selfishness.

Focus Points...

What a beautiful thing, GOD, to give thanks, to sing an anthem to you, the High God!
PSALM 92:1 MSG

Everything God made is good, and nothing should be refused if it is accepted with thanks.
1 TIMOTHY 4:4 NCV

Oh, give thanks to the God of gods! For His mercy endures forever.
PSALM 136:2 NKJV

Enter into His gates with thanksgiving, and into His courts with praise. Be thankful to Him, and bless His name.
PSALM 100:4 NKJV

what really counts

Let us continually offer the sacrifice of praise to God, that is, the fruit of our lips, giving thanks to His name.
HEBREWS 13:15 NKJV

The unthankful heart . . . discovers no mercies; but the thankful heart . . . will find, in every hour, some heavenly blessing.

HENRY WARD BEECHER

A thankful heart is not only the greatest virtue, but the parent of all other virtues.

CICERO

189

Peace and Happiness
What Are You Waiting For?

Make the most of every chance
you get. These are desperate times!
EPHESIANS 5:16 MSG

Everybody knows at least one story about a midlife crisis. The man who quits a successful career and moves to the mountains to write poetry. The man who leaves his wife of thirty years and moves in with a woman half his age. The man who trades in his serviceable Buick for a red two-seater. Sometimes a midlife crisis is minor and harmless. Sometimes it's disastrous, shattering many lives. But where does a midlife crisis come from? Why is it so common? A midlife crisis occurs when a man begins to believe that his best chance for happiness is behind him.

A midlife crisis is the result of frustrated desire. You spend your boyhood and youth and young manhood believing that the fulfillment of your desires will happen when you achieve some future attainment—when you finish school or get married or get the right job or the right promotion. Then you wake up one day and instead of being frustrated that your chance for happiness hasn't gotten here yet, you're hit with the sense that your chance for happiness was back there in the past somewhere. You feel that your life was what happened to you while you were waiting for your life to get started. It can be a terrifying feeling, and men react to it in some pretty unusual ways.

But it doesn't have to be that way. The truth is, your best chance for happiness is right now. Purpose and meaning are to be found in a relationship with the God who made you. He is as present now as He will ever be. "The LORD is near to all who call upon Him, to all who call upon Him in truth. He will fulfill the desire of those who fear Him" (Psalm 145:18–19 NKJV). If your desires are frustrated, perhaps it's time you got some new desires. If you desire God, you're going to get what you want. Draw near to Him, and he'll draw near to you.

As you get serious about your relationship with God, your career, your home life, and your hobbies take on more significance, not less. When you no longer expect the things of earth to give your life meaning and ultimate happiness, you can enjoy them for such happiness and pleasure as they do provide. That's abundant life. So what are you waiting for?

Peace and Happiness
What Are You Waiting For?

What Matters Most...

◎ Seizing the day. Now is the time to get serious about finding happiness in God.

◎ Seeking God. There's no other place to find lasting peace and happiness.

◎ Desiring the right things. If you desire the things of God, your desire won't be frustrated.

◎ Acknowledging God's blessings. Dwell on what's good about the life God has given you.

◎ Making the most of what you have. God has given you everything you need.

What **Doesn't** Matter...

◎ Excuses. If you aren't happy, don't go looking for someone else to blame. Seek God, the only One who can make you happy.

◎ The belief that your best chance at happiness is in the future. The time is now.

◎ The belief that your best chance for happiness is already past. The time is now.

◎ The marketers' plan for your life. Material goods won't give you peace or happiness.

◎ The inner voice of defeat. If God is for you, who can be against you?

Focus Points...

Since everything here today might well be gone tomorrow, do you see how essential it is to live a holy life?
2 PETER 3:11 MSG

Today, if you will hear His voice, do not harden your hearts.
HEBREWS 4:7 NKJV

I [Jesus] have come that they may have life, and that they may have it more abundantly.
JOHN 10:10 NKJV

Choose for yourselves this day whom you will serve.
JOSHUA 24:15 NKJV

This is the day that the LORD has made. Let us rejoice and be glad today!
PSALM 118:24 NCV

what really counts

The grand essentials to happiness in this life are something to do, something to love, and something to hope for.
JOSEPH ADDISON

He who has no vision of eternity will never get a true hold of time.
THOMAS CARLYLE

What Matters Most to Me About
Peace and Happiness

True peace and happiness cannot be found in what's going on around you. It's up to you to make sure your thoughts and attitudes are filled with godly wisdom. The first step in that direction is a thankful heart.

◎ *Look at 1 Peter 3:11. What does Peter tell you to turn away from? What does he command you to do?*

_____

_____

_____

_____

_____

_____

_____

_____

◎ *Write about a day when something good happened to that made you happy. What about the opposite? How can you find joy that is not based on your circumstances?*

_____

_____

_____

_____

_____

_____

_____

◎ *Do you ever feel like you are whining to God? What about? How can you turn those complaints into gratitude? What are some things you are thankful for today?*

_____

_____

_____

_____

_____

_____

_____

_____

◎ *Name two things about the life of Christ that demonstrate His attitude of joyfulness despite difficult circumstances. What can you learn from Him?*

_____

_____

_____

_____

_____

_____

_____

_____

_____

> True contentment is a thing as active as agriculture. It is the power of getting out of any situation all that there is in it. It is arduous and it is rare.
> G. K. CHESTERTON

PERSONAL GROWTH
An Introduction

> I, the prisoner of the Lord, implore you to walk in a manner worthy of the calling with which you have been called.
>
> EPHESIANS 4:1 NASB

what really counts

When the word *virtue* came into the English language, it meant something like "manly courage" or "manly strength." It was closely linked to a soldierly sort of courage and initiative—the power to make good things happen. In the intervening years, the word *virtue* has taken on a more feminine connotation. It has come to be almost synonymous with chastity or virginity—an important facet of moral excellence to be sure, but one defined by what you won't do, not by what you can or will do.

The word *virtue* serves as a reminder that true manliness has long been associated with moral excellence, even if the idea seems unusual in a culture where the stock male sitcom characters seem all to be either hen-pecked losers or men behaving badly. In many homes and many relationships, men have abdicated their moral responsibility toward the people around them. But God's blueprint for manhood has always combined strength and kindness in a life marked by integrity, initiative, and love.

Virtue works from the inside out. It begins with your thought life and works its way into your actions. It defines your relationships. It expresses itself in humility, but also in a confidence that finds its basis in the God who never fails. A virtuous man is free from self-doubt, self-consciousness, and self-promotion. He is free to follow after his life's purpose. A virtuous man is gracious and forgiving. He knows what God is like. He shows what God is like.

> Character is like a tree and reputation like its shadow. The shadow is what we think of it; the tree is the real thing.
>
> ABRAHAM LINCOLN

Personal Growth
You Go First

Here is a simple, rule-of-thumb guide for behavior: Ask yourself what you want people to do for you, then grab the initiative and do it for them. Add up God's Law and Prophets and this is what you get.

MATTHEW 7:12 MSG

what really counts

It wasn't a shining moment in the history of manhood. Adam and Eve were standing in the Garden of Eden, having just polished off the Forbidden Fruit. They had pieced together fig leaves to cover their nakedness when they heard God coming. God asked Adam a very simple question: "Have you eaten from the tree of which I commanded you that you should not eat?" It was Adam's chance to be a man, to take responsibility. It was a simple yes-no question, but Adam blew it. "The woman whom You gave to be with me, she gave me of the tree, and I ate" (Genesis 3:11–12 NKJV). A simple yes would have sufficed, but instead, Adam started pointing fingers. It's the woman's fault, Adam said. It isn't just her fault, but the fault of the God who gave her to him.

Adam's first sin wasn't eating the apple. Before that, his sin was a retreat into passivity. When Eve held out the fruit to him, he had the chance to take charge of the situation, to help her get back on track, lead her to ask God for forgiveness—to do something besides passively taking the apple and meekly joining her in her sin. When confronted by God, he had a second chance to be a man, but he chose instead to portray himself as a victim. His wife was frightened and ashamed. She needed a husband to comfort her, to speak up for her, to love her. But he blamed her; even worse, he blamed God for creating her. When Eve most needed Adam to step up and be a man, he chose passivity, and so failed her.

Passivity can be a slow poison in your relationships. The laws of inertia aren't on your side when it comes to interpersonal relationships. True manliness is the willingness to set the tone in your daily interactions—a tone of godliness, honesty, integrity, justice. Take the initiative in your relationships. It's up to you to be the first to apologize, the first to forgive, the first to confront in love. Don't leave room to blame your shortcomings on anyone else, and certainly not on anyone who is weaker than you, or someone who looks to you for leadership. You deal every day with the aftermath of Adam's passivity, but the effects are reversible if you're willing to submit to God's plan for your relationships.

Personal Growth
You Go First

What Matters Most...

◎ Putting God first. If that relationship is right, your other relationships will improve.

◎ Taking responsibility. Your actions are your actions. Don't leave room to blame them on anybody else.

◎ Going more than halfway. In any relationship, meeting the other person halfway isn't nearly enough. Go all the way to their doorstep if you need to.

◎ Being a leader. Passivity in your relationships is a recipe for disaster.

◎ Loving. Let all your actions toward other people be motivated by love.

What **Doesn't** Matter...

◎ The blame game. Shifting blame is unmanly. Take responsibility for your own actions, and give others the benefit of the doubt whenever you can.

◎ Self-protection. If you're constantly covering your own backside, you won't be much good to anybody.

◎ Self-pity. Focus on the ways you've been blessed, not on your misfortunes.

◎ Self-absorption. Being a leader is about reaching out to others, not retreating into yourself.

Focus Points...

If it is possible, as much as depends on you, live peaceably with all men.
ROMANS 12:18 NKJV

Outdo one another in showing honor.
ROMANS 12:10 HCSB

Don't hurt your friend, don't blame your neighbor.
PSALM 15:3 MSG

People's own foolishness ruins their lives, but in their minds they blame the LORD.
PROVERBS 19:3 NCV

It's easy to see a smudge on your neighbor's face and be oblivious to the ugly sneer on your own. Do you have the nerve to say, "Let me wash your face for you," when your own face is distorted by contempt?
MATTHEW 7:3–4 MSG

what really counts

The price of greatness is responsibility.

WINSTON CHURCHILL

One of the annoying things about believing in free will and individual responsibility is the difficulty in finding someone to blame your troubles on. And when you do find someone, it's remarkable how often their picture turns up on your driver's license.

P. J. O'ROURKE

Personal Growth
As a Man Thinks, So He Is

> Be careful what you think, because your thoughts run your life.
>
> PROVERBS 4:23 NCV

what really counts

The enemies of Jesus accused him of having too low a view of the Law. They must have missed the Sermon on the Mount, for there Jesus ratcheted up the claims of the Law to a level that not even the Pharisees, with all their rules and regulations, could have imagined. He took the Law, which had always been applied to the outer life of actions and words, and applied it to the inner life—the thoughts and little obsessions that nobody sees but you and God. The Old Testament Law forbade murder. Jesus said that anyone who harbors anger against another without cause is guilty of murder. The Old Testament Law forbade adultery. Jesus said that any man who lusts after a woman is guilty of adultery.

That's an alarming thought. Who isn't guilty of anger and lust? Yet there it is, in red letters in your Bible. It's human nature to judge a person by what's on the outside—what they do or say or how they look. We expect to be judged that way, but God sees who you are on the inside, at your very core. That inner life, that thought life is the real you, not the cleaned-up, well-dressed outside that you present to the world.

But as always with the Gospel, the bad news is quickly followed by good news. God sees your inner self, but it's also your inner self that He reaches into and changes. If you are in Christ you are a new man, from the inside out. As God completes the work He has begun in you, He conforms your mind to the mind of Christ. You begin to think His thoughts after Him.

A life of integrity begins with your thought life. You can't control the wrong thoughts that drift into your head, but you can keep them from taking root. How? By so filling your mind with the things of God that there's little room for the things that would draw you away. By dwelling on things that build you up rather than tearing you down. "Finally, brethren, whatever things are true, whatever things are noble, whatever things are just, whatever things are pure, whatever things are lovely, whatever things are of good report, if there is any virtue and if there is anything praiseworthy—meditate on these things" (Philippians 4:8 NKJV). That's the kind of thought life that's worth living.

Personal Growth
As a Man Thinks, So He Is

What Matters Most...

◎ The things your mind dwells on. That's who you are, really.

◎ The things you do. What starts in your head eventually makes its way to your outer life.

◎ Mental purity. It takes effort to cultivate a pure thought life. Take care what you put into your head.

◎ Sanctification. God is at work, renewing you from the inside out.

◎ A mind full of noble, lovely thoughts. It's your protection against mental corruption.

What Doesn't Matter...

◎ Your outward appearance. God looks at the heart.

◎ Fleeting thoughts. As long as they don't find a place to perch, they won't do you lasting harm.

◎ Past hypocrisies. You can make a new start.

◎ Unrealistic expectations. There's no getting around the fact that wrong thoughts will enter your mind from the outside. The question is, what will you do with them once they've entered the lobby of your mind?

◎ Self-punishment. Focus on filling your mind with good things, not punishing yourself for your failures.

Focus Points...

What people say with their mouths comes from the way they think; these are the things that make people unclean. Out of the mind come evil thoughts, murder, adultery, sexual sins, stealing, lying, and speaking evil of others. These things make people unclean; eating with unwashed hands does not make them unclean.
MATTHEW 15:18–20 NCV

The thoughts of the righteous are right, but the counsels of the wicked are deceitful.
PROVERBS 12:5 NKJV

People with their minds set on you, you keep completely whole, steady on their feet, because they keep at it and don't quit.
ISAIAH 26:3 MSG

what really counts

Who can say, "I have made my heart clean, I am pure from my sin"?
PROVERBS 20:9 NKJV

What you are must always displease you, if you would attain that which you are not.

SAINT AUGUSTINE

What we plant in the soil of contemplation, we shall reap in the harvest of action.

MEISTER ECKHART

Personal Growth
Living Grace

> It is by God's grace that you have been saved through faith. It is not the result of your own efforts, but God's gift, so that no one can boast about it.
>
> EPHESIANS 2:8–9 GNT

what really counts

You walk from your car to the front door of your house after a busy day at work, and there you see it: an expensive, chewed-up tennis shoe. You feel your blood pressure begin to rise a bit as your realize *once again,* your son left his shoes outside and the dog got hold of one. You're not mad, you're furious. You feel like you have every right to be angry.

Or do you? There's not much point arguing whether or not you have the right or not. God wants you to hand over your rights to Him, and that includes the right to vent your anger. Maybe you spent your summer slaving away at the office while your partner spent several weeks at the beach or in the mountains. He had the nerve to send you those smiling digital pictures! Or maybe it's that daily afternoon commute that gets your blood boiling as you race home to squeeze in some downtime before dinner. You may feel the highways are teeming with insensitive, careless drivers who seem to enjoy cutting you off mile after mile.

In the same way that God overlooks your offenses and extends grace, you should offer this same grace in your daily relationships. You may not *feel* like forgiving someone who has wronged you, but as you mature in your Christian faith, you'll learn to love others through grace received from Christ. Those little irritations that cause you to want to lose control are God's way of testing your character. Will you react according to the ways of the flesh, or according to the divine interaction of the Holy Spirit?

If you try to extend grace and love to others on your own, you'll fall short every time. It's impossible to live the perfect live without God's Spirit living through you. Your prayer should be that you'll become less so that He may become more, loving and working through you. You are held captive to your sin nature until you find freedom in obedience to Christ. What a joy it is to be released from that prison! David felt the pleasure of God when he penned these words, "I run in the path of your commands, for you have set my heart free" (Psalm 119:32 NIV). Give thanks to God when you have a heart that is free enough to offer His supernatural grace!

Personal Growth
Living Grace

What Matters Most...

◎ Extending grace to others because God is gracious to you.

◎ Loving and forgiving others when you feel like you have a right to be angry.

◎ Submitting to the will of God in all matters of the heart.

◎ Listening to the quiet, gentle voice of the Spirit who prods you to step beyond your self-limitations.

◎ Running in the path of God's commands that will set your heart free.

What Doesn't Matter...

◎ Your feelings. Let go of how you feel and focus on what God commands you to do.

◎ Your memories. God tells you to forgive seventy times seven—even if the person repeats that same mistake over and over!

◎ Your personality. Contrary to popular beliefs, you are not trapped in a personality when you let God's Spirit renew your mind and change you.

◎ Your past mistakes. God forgives you each time and wipes your slate clean.

◎ Your stubbornness. Ask God to help you extend grace and offer forgiveness to someone who has offended you.

Focus Points...

The Lord laughs at those who laugh at him, but he gives grace to those who are not proud.
Proverbs 3:34 NCV

The Word became flesh, and dwelt among us, and we saw His glory, glory as of the only begotten from the Father, full of grace and truth.
John 1:14 NASB

God in his gracious kindness declares us not guilty. He has done this through Christ Jesus, who has freed us by taking away our sins.
Romans 3:24 NLT

Sin shall not have dominion over you, for you are not under law but under grace.
Romans 6:14 NKJV

what really counts

The important thing is that we be able to look back and say, "Well, I'm not where I hope to be someday, but thank God I am different from what I was."

J. I. Packer

If you feel inadequate, turn to Christ. Confess your need, and find restoration through his grace. This is the heart of his redemption—he heals us and gives us new life.

Richard Halverson

Personal Growth
Humility

> Take my yoke and put it on you, and
> learn from me, because I am gentle and
> humble in spirit; and you will find rest.
> MATTHEW 11:29 GNT

what really counts

If you're like most men, when you stop to take a look in your closet, you've probably built up a halfway decent wardrobe. All those gifts over the years have added up, and you have a shirt for every occasion. You have crisp, collared dress shirts handy for those formal church and work events. You can't live without your weekend cotton favorites, perfect for flipping burgers on the grill or a day on the greens. Then there are your grass-cutting, ball-playing, lounging-around T-shirts. If your collection can survive your wife's ruthless spring cleaning attacks, then you're set. Ah . . . you have it all.

But what about your spiritual wardrobe? God doesn't look at what you're wearing on the outside; he's busy looking at your heart. He'd like you to be clothed in humility. It's one of His favorite qualities. Peter tells you to "clothe yourselves with humility toward one another, because, 'God opposes the proud but gives grace to the humble'" (1 Peter 5:5 NIV). So, what does a humble man look like?

A proud guy gets a promotion at work and tells all his colleagues he knew it was coming because he's single-handedly increased profits since he was hired. But a humble man says, "I give God all the glory for my success." An arrogant guy can't wait to get ahead of the Joneses—he's the first to trade in for a bigger house, a flashier car, maybe even a younger wife if she can keep him feeling like the macho man he believes himself to be. In contrast, a humble man lives beneath his means, shares his blessings with others less fortunate, and keeps walking the straight and narrow path with the wife of his youth.

Just how important is humility to God? Jesus modeled it over and over again for His disciples. He washed their dusty feet and asked them to do the same for others. One day, He hiked up a mountain with Peter, James, and John to give them a brief glimpse of His heavenly glory. For an awesome moment, His face shone as brightly as the sun, and His plain robe flashed white with brilliance. But when the experience ended, Jesus returned to His example of humbling Himself before earthly authorities. If the Lord of the heavens dressed Himself in robes of humility, then it's no stretch to imagine He wants you to do the same.

Personal Growth
Humility

What Matters Most...

◎ Remembering the complete humility of the Lord Jesus.

◎ Trying to walk in Christ's footsteps in the way you serve others.

◎ Being willing to serve in the lowliest of places, in same way Christ washed His disciples' feet.

◎ Realizing that being humble is an act of obedience, and is a sign of character growth.

◎ Loving others who exhibit pride, and knowing that they are still journeying toward spiritual maturity.

What Doesn't Matter...

◎ Self-righteous beliefs. All your goodness comes from your heavenly father.

◎ Pride in past accomplishments. You can't take anything to heaven with you but your faith, and the faith of those whose lives you touch.

◎ Works. They will not earn you any points with God. Everything you accomplish is because He enabled you.

◎ Jealousy toward others. The comparison trap is one sure way you can lose your joy.

◎ Inability to be humble on your own. Pray that you'll learn to live in the light of His glory.

Focus Points...

When pride comes, then comes disgrace, but with humility comes wisdom.
PROVERBS 11:2 NIV

All these things my hand has made, and so all these things are mine, says the LORD. But this is the one to whom I will look, to the humble and contrite in spirit, who trembles at my word.
ISAIAH 66:2 NRSV

All of you, leaders and followers alike, are to be down to earth with each other, for—God has had it with the proud, but takes delight in just plain people.
1 PETER 5:5 MSG

Do nothing from selfishness or empty conceit, but with humility of mind regard one another as more important than yourselves.
PHILIPPIANS 2:3 NASB

what really counts

Our friendship with Jesus is based on the new life He created in us . . . It is a life that is completely humble, pure, and devoted to God.

OSWALD CHAMBERS

The first thing I do every morning is to get on my knees and acknowledge Christ's presence within me and his lordship of my life.

BILL BRIGHT

Personal Growth
What Do You Want?

As the deer pants for the water brooks,
so pants my soul for You, O God.

PSALM 42:1 NKJV

When you were a little boy at Christmas, it was easy making out your wish list. You may have sat in Santa's lap going over your deepest wants, but you said them extra loud, just to be sure your parents standing nearby wouldn't miss a word. Maybe you asked for a new bike . . . a hamster . . . or your two front teeth. Those were the easy days of figuring out what you needed to make you happy.

Now, it's gotten more complicated. You have two goals you're pushing toward. On one side, you're aching to rise up in your career, to establish yourself as an authority in your field. You feel like you've worked hard, and your time has come to earn more income and feel control over the world around you. Or maybe you've already reached the top, but you have to put in the hours to prove you deserve to be where you are. Meanwhile, you spend the other two-thirds of your life at home—eating, drinking, and sleeping with the family

214

God has blessed you with. They stretch and pull at you too, needing more of you than you feel like you have to offer.

Pastor Andy Stanley struggled with this issue when he was starting his new church in suburban Atlanta. His financial and staff resources were stretched thin, and he felt like he needed to oversee every step of the growth process. Meanwhile, his wife was at home with two young children and pregnant with a third. She had a request of him. She asked him if he could please start coming home from work every day at 4:00 p.m. At first Stanley thought this was an impossible task. How could a pastor only work 45 hours a week? He wondered if others would look down on him for placing his family in front of his career.

After much prayer, he realized that many of the families who sought his counsel were on the brink of divorce primarily because the men spent too much time away from home. So Andy followed his wife's request. What happened to that fledgling handful of fellowshippers? His congregation grew rapidly to more than 15,000 people, causing him to have to expand and build a second campus. He gives this advice, "In choosing to put your family first, you have brought your priorities in line with those of your heavenly Father."

Personal Growth
What Do You Want?

What Matters Most...

◎ Trusting God to fill in the gaps when you order your priorities His way: God, family, career.

◎ Being patient as God works out the details of how you will live out your priorities.

◎ Taking good care of your mental and physical health so that you can give your best to your workplace and home.

◎ Desiring a deep relationship with God over all else in your life.

◎ Reading Scriptures to find strength from examples of God's people who chose to follow him over pleasing others.

What **Doesn't** Matter...

◎ Feeling guilty that you're having to balance your time between work and home.

◎ Comparing your career progress to others who sacrifice everything for material attainment.

◎ Putting bigger dreams on hold while you're busy raising young children. They're only teachable for a short period of time.

◎ Wishing there were more hours in the day so that you could get more done. Let God have control of your schedule.

Focus Points...

Delight yourself also in the LORD, and He shall give you the desires of your heart.
PSALM 37:4 NKJV

Whom have I in heaven but you? And earth has nothing I desire besides you.
PSALM 73:25 NIV

Those who are according to the flesh set their minds on the things of the flesh, but those who are according to the Spirit, the things of the Spirit.
ROMANS 8:5 NASB

Stay away from lusts which tempt young people. Pursue what has God's approval. Pursue faith, love, and peace together with those who worship the Lord with a pure heart.
2 TIMOTHY 2:22 GOD'S WORD

what really counts

When you eliminate certain options, it's amazing how resourceful you become. Conviction eliminates options.
ANDY STANLEY

Give me one hundred preachers who fear nothing but sin, and desire nothing but God, and I care not a straw whether they be clergymen or laymen; such alone will shake the gates of hell and set up the kingdom of heaven on earth.
JOHN WESLEY

Personal Growth
Freeing Others, Freeing Yourself

Be even-tempered, content with second place, quick to forgive an offense. Forgive as quickly and completely as the Master forgave you.

COLOSSIANS 3:13 MSG

what really counts

Think about what it's like to make a bad loan or to extend credit to someone who never pays you back. You ask, you demand, you threaten, but to no avail. At some point you realize that you'll never get your money back. Your efforts to collect are more of a burden on you than they are on the person who owes you. So you write it off at last and get a small break on your taxes and hopefully a little peace of mind.

Every time a person sins against you, he incurs a moral debt. That's why some translations of the Lord's Prayer say "forgive us our debts as we forgive our debtors." The problem is, that debt can't truly be repaid. Even when a person is genuinely sorry, he can't unsay cruel words he's said or totally heal the hurt he's caused. In the end, when a person has wronged you, it's up to you to clear the tab. His apologies, his contrition, his efforts to make it up to you might make it easier for you to write off the debt, but it's still up to you.

What about those people who don't even try to make it up to you? It's not nearly so easy to release those people. Why should you release them? Here's why: Because in a case like that, you're the one who needs to be set free, not them. As with any other bad debt, the effort to collect it is more of a burden on you than on the debtor. While you're composing debt collection letters in your head and imagining scenarios involving baseball bats and busted kneecaps, the person who wronged you is going about his business. If you're marinating in bitterness, you're the one whose soul shrivels. It may not seem fair, but it's the way the world works. It's better to write off the bad debt, take your tax break, and move on.

It's not easy to forgive, but it's easier when you consider how much you've been forgiven. All sin is ultimately sin against God. When you couldn't begin to pay your sin-debt, God paid it for you in the person of Christ. Next time you pull out your ledger to do a little moral accounting, take account of that transaction before you start trying to collect on the debts other people owe you.

Personal Growth
Freeing Others, Freeing Yourself

What Matters Most...

◎ The forgiveness that you have received from God. This is your motivation to forgive others.

◎ A loving spirit. Love doesn't keep track of wrongs.

◎ Keeping yourself free. Forgiveness is the best way to keep from enslaving yourself.

◎ Freeing others. You're the one who is really set free.

◎ Keeping a clear conscience. Ask forgiveness of anyone you've wronged.

What **Doesn't** Matter...

◎ The desire for payback. Being free is better than getting back.

◎ The size of the wrong done. Big or small, your best bet is to let it go.

◎ How long ago it happened. Years ago, or earlier today, now is the time to forgive.

◎ Whose fault it is. Don't keep a ledger.

◎ Pride. Pride is no reason to enslave yourself.

Focus Points...

Forgive us our debts, as we forgive our debtors.
MATTHEW 6:12 NKJV

Be kind and loving to each other, and forgive each other just as God forgave you in Christ.
EPHESIANS 4:32 NCV

If he sins against you seven times in a day, and seven times in a day returns to you, saying, "I repent," you shall forgive him.
LUKE 17:4 NKJV

Happy is the person whose sins are forgiven, whose wrongs are pardoned.
PSALM 32:1 NCV

what really counts

Whenever you stand praying, if you have anything against anyone, forgive him, that your Father in heaven may also forgive you your trespasses.
MARK 11:25 NKJV

Forgiveness does not mean ignoring what has been done or putting a false label on an evil act. It means, rather, that the evil act no longer remains as a barrier to the relationship.

MARTIN LUTHER KING JR.

To carry a grudge is like being stung to death by one bee.
WILLIAM H. WALTON

221

Personal Growth
Strong and Courageous

Haven't I commanded you? Strength! Courage!
Don't be timid; don't get discouraged. GOD,
your God, is with you every step you take.

JOSHUA 1:9 MSG

what really counts

Some say he stood defiantly, arm upraised toward heaven; others say he knelt humbly as in prayer. Although the details are sketchy, one thing is clear: On April 16, 1521, Martin Luther showed the true meaning of the word *courage*. It was on this day that he boldly faced the German emperor at the Imperial Diet of Worms. Confronted the false doctrines of a corrupt church, he had gone where no man before him had ever dared to go. His courageous stand, the beginning of the Protestant Reformation, changed the world forever. Luther found his courage from Scripture. As a young monk, when he read the verse, "The righteous will live by faith" (Romans 1:17 NIV), a lightning bolt streaked through his soul as he realized that man is accountable to God alone.

On that historical April day, Luther said, "My conscience is captive to the Word of God . . . To go against conscience is neither right nor safe. God help me. Amen." He was then declared an outlaw, and anyone who kidnapped or killed him could escape unpunished. But God protected Luther and allowed him to dwell in safety and continue hammering the world with his writings. His life goes beyond an inspiring lesson in church history. It hits you in the heart when you realize God wants you to have this same kind of courage.

In the same way that God implored Joshua not to be timid or discouraged when entering the Promised Land, He calls you to show courage confronting evil in your world. What about that coworker who enjoys sending you seedy e-mail jokes? They fill your mind with unwholesome images, but it's easier to press delete than to ask him to stop. It takes courage to approach your boss when he schedules you for a business trip the same week that you've promised to go camping with your son's Boy Scout troop.

In 2003, a chief justice in Montgomery, Alabama, exhibited great courage when he went against court orders to remove the Ten Commandments from the rotunda in his court building. He believed the laws of the nation were based on God's Word. Although he was ridiculed and lost the battle, his example stands as an encouragement to continue upholding the truths you believe in. Ask God to help you be a man of courage and seek ways to be captive to your conscience, which is the Holy Spirit's way of empowering you.

Personal Growth
Strong and Courageous

What Matters Most...

◎ Abiding daily in the Word of God, so that you will be familiar with biblical examples of courage.

◎ Being captive to the Holy Spirit, who speaks to you through your conscience.

◎ Admitting your fears to God, so that He alone will enable you to act with courage.

◎ Honoring God with your life by being an example to others.

◎ Acknowledging God as the source of your strength and courage when you attempt to stand up for your faith.

What Doesn't Matter...

◎ Feeling alone. God is with you and will strengthen you to do what you know is right.

◎ Your fears. The psalmist wrote, "The fear of the LORD is the beginning of wisdom" (Psalm 111:10 NIV). No other kind of fear matters.

◎ What others think. As long as you have your focus on God and His Word, then the words of others don't hold you captive.

◎ Your lack of experience. If you've never confronted evil before, you may not know how things will turn out, but God's plan is for you to follow His ways.

Focus Points...

Act with courage, and may the LORD be with those who do well.
2 CHRONICLES 19:11 NIV

Jesus spoke to them and said, "Take heart, it is I; do not be afraid."
MATTHEW 14:27 NRSV

Be alert. Be firm in the Christian faith. Be courageous and strong.
1 CORINTHIANS 16:13 GOD'S WORD

I urge you to take heart, for there will be no loss of life among you, but only of the ship.
ACTS 27:22 NKJV

what really counts

Christ, the faithful Son, was in charge of the entire household. And we are God's household, if we keep up our courage and remain confident in our hope in Christ.
HEBREWS 3:6 NLT

Never undertake anything for which you wouldn't have the courage to ask the blessing of heaven.

G. C. LICHTENBERG

Hope has two beautiful daughters Their names are anger and courage; anger at the way things are, and courage to see that they do not remain the way they are.

SAINT AUGUSTINE

Personal Growth
True Reflection

Those who are pure in their thinking are happy, because they will be with God.

MATTHEW 5:8 NCV

what really counts

One Sabbath day in ancient Jerusalem, two views of holiness came into collision. At the healing pool of Bethesda, Jesus encountered a lame man who had waited there for years in hopes of being healed. Jesus asked the man if he wanted to get well. The old-fashioned language of the King James Version actually gets closest to the original Greek: "Wilt thou be whole?" (John 5:6). The man had been broken for thirty-eight years; he surely felt like half a man. Jesus offered to make him whole. The lame man leapt at the chance. Jesus healed him and sent him away carrying the bedroll he on which he had languished for years.

That's when the poor fellow ran into the Pharisees. They didn't seem very interested in the fact that a lame man could now walk. Instead, they scolded him for carrying his bedroll on the Sabbath, which was technically against the law. The Pharisees were sticklers for their notion of holiness, but that was nothing more than a set of rules and checklists. They weren't holy men because they weren't whole men. There was obviously something missing in men who could see a man made whole after thirty-eight years of brokenness and scold him instead of rejoicing with him.

A broken man made whole. That's the essence of holiness, not a set of rules. In English, the word *holy* comes from the same root as the word *whole*. A holy life is a life characterized by wholeness, in which the spiritual is fully integrated with the day-to-day. Jesus told the lame man, "Thou art made whole: sin no more" (John 5:14 KJV). The power to live a godly life comes from the work of Christ that makes you whole.

In your brokenness, you were unable to reflect God's image very accurately. But as the fragments of your self are collected and pieced together, the image of God reflected in you is more and more recognizable. God gives His people "all things that pertain to life and godliness" (2 Peter 1:3 NKJV). There's wholeness for you: Whatever you lacked, God has supplied. He hasn't supplied it merely so you can follow the rules. He has supplied it so you can be a whole man, a real man—one who loves even the unlovely, who fights for what is right, who brings the truths of God to bear on the world around him.

Personal Growth
True Reflection

What Matters Most...

- Reflecting the image of God. Holiness shows the world what God looks like.

- Being whole. God can put the pieces of your self back together.

- Following Christ. Obedience is the proper response of a man made whole.

- Integrity. A holy life is one in which your spiritual life matches up with your day-to-day life.

- Desire. If you desire holiness, you will be made holy.

What Doesn't Matter...

- An ever-growing list of rules. Faith, not rule-keeping, is the basis of holiness.

- Your moral strength, or lack of it. It takes strength from outside of you—God's strength—to make you holy.

- The criticism of legalists. You're accountable to God first, not to other people.

- The ridicule of the worldly. God's wisdom isn't the world's wisdom.

- The depth of your brokenness. The lame man hadn't walked in thirty-eight years, but he was made whole.

Focus Points...

Anyone who claims to be intimate with God ought to live the same kind of life Jesus lived.
1 JOHN 2:6 MSG

Do not be conformed to this world, but be transformed by the renewing of your mind, that you may prove what is that good and acceptable and perfect will of God.
ROMANS 12:2 NKJV

God hasn't invited us into a disorderly, unkempt life but into something holy and beautiful—as beautiful on the inside as the outside.
1 THESSALONIANS 4:7 MSG

God has made you his friends again. He did this through Christ's death in the body so that he might bring you into God's presence as people who are holy, with no wrong, and with nothing of which God can judge you guilty.
COLOSSIANS 1:22 NCV

what really counts

A holy life will produce the deepest impression. Lighthouses blow no horns; they only shine.

D. L. MOODY

Holy has the same root as wholly, it means complete. A man is not complete in spiritual stature if all his mind, heart, soul, and strength are not given to God.

R. J. STEWART

What Matters Most to Me About
Personal Growth

If you are in Christ, you have become righteous in God's sight. Now you're becoming what you have already become. You are being shaped into a person who looks more like Christ, as God finishes the work He began in you.

◎ *A solid and true life is lived from the inside out. What are the places in your life where the outside—the part of you that everyone else sees—doesn't match up with the inside? How can you bring outside and inside into alignment?*

_____

_____

_____

_____

_____

_____

_____

_____

◎ *Reflect on Philippians 4:8. What are some true, noble, reputable, authentic, and compelling things you can dwell on? Be specific.*

_____

_____

_____

_____

_____

_____

_____

⊚ *What are the areas of your life where you need to show more grace to other people?*

_____

_____

_____

_____

_____

_____

_____

_____

_____

⊚ *How do you define manliness? Where in your life do you need to be more manly?*

_____

_____

_____

_____

_____

_____

_____

_____

_____

_____

To starve to death is a small thing, but to lose one's integrity is a great one.

CHINESE PROVERB

PRAYER

An Introduction

> You will seek Me and find Me, when you search for Me with all your heart.
>
> JEREMIAH 29:13 NKJV

what really counts

John Piper once wrote that a prayerless Christian is like a bus driver straining on his own to push his bus out of a rut because he doesn't realize that Clark Kent is on board. God Almighty, the Maker of heaven and earth, is near at hand and ready to intervene on your behalf. To pray is to avail yourself of that incredible power. He delights to answer the prayers of His people, to unleash His power on their behalf. Yet Christians often strain and struggle to do in their own strength what God would happily do for them if they would only ask.

The essence of prayer is a turning away from your self—your own resources, your own worries, your own doubts—and toward God. It's relinquishing control—

or, more to the point, relinquishing the illusion of control—and resting in God's faithfulness. You may not be entirely comfortable with that idea. You may have a problem giving up control. If so, you may have a problem with prayer.

God has already said yes to you. He has said yes on all the big things. Yes, He loves you. Yes, He wants the best for you. Yes, He can make it happen. Yes, you can come boldly into His presence and make your requests known. When you come before him, you are stepping into a world of yes. Sure, there are times when God says no, but only in the service of a larger yes. So pray without ceasing. Pray without fear.

I have been driven many times to my knees by the overwhelming conviction that I had nowhere else to go.

ABRAHAM LINCOLN

Prayer
An Attitude of Prayer

Pray without ceasing.

1 THESSALONIANS 5:17

Paul urged the Thessalonians to "pray without ceasing." How do you do that? You're a busy man. You have things to do. You can't be bowing your head and closing your eyes all day every day. Obviously Paul must have been talking about something else when he said to pray without ceasing. He was talking about a habit or attitude of Godward thinking. Prayer without ceasing means shaping your thoughts into prayers, directing your thoughts toward God rather than letting them dissolve into the air after you've thought them. Every little worry is transformed into a quick prayer for God's help and guidance. Every gratitude is turned into a prayer of thanksgiving to the God who is always blessing. Every joy becomes a prayer of praise to the Giver of all joy. Every moment of anger or lust or greed dissolves into a prayer of confession and repentance, a reminder that you need God constantly.

To pray without ceasing is to give your thoughts a life outside your head, to reach out constantly to the God who delights to draw near to you. As you develop that attitude, you begin to look more like God. As your thoughts become prayers, you start to think more like God. Just as importantly, as you develop the habit of Godward thinking, you also learn the habit of hearing God's voice. Because prayer, like any other conversation, goes two ways.

That's not to say that you shouldn't also block out time each day for serious head-bowed, eyes-closed prayer—time when you aren't doing anything else besides praying. Pray that way too. Just be careful that your prayer time doesn't become an activity you can check off your to-do list for the day. Morning prayers should kick off a day marked by an attitude of prayer. Evening prayers should give shape and structure to a day's worth of thought-prayers.

To pray without ceasing is to realize that God is as close as the air you breathe. A prayerful attitude constantly punches through the seeming barrier between the material world and the world of the spirit. It reminds you that there is more to the world than meets the eye. It gives you a spiritual vantage point from which to view all of everyday living. Do you want to walk by the Spirit? Then pray without ceasing.

Prayer
An Attitude of Prayer

What Matters Most...

◎ Knowing that God is near. He's as close as the air around you.

◎ Reaching out to God. He cares about every aspect of your life.

◎ Getting outside of yourself. Prayer stretches you. Prayer encourages new attitudes.

◎ Knowing the spiritual world to be as real as the material world.

◎ Praying without ceasing. It's a lifestyle. It's a habit as wonderful to the soul as air is to the body.

What **Doesn't** Matter...

◎ Self-absorption. An attitude of prayer will overcome it. Pray for other people.

◎ Self-consciousness. God accepts you just the way you are.

◎ Self-reliance. An attitude of prayer is a recognition that God is all your hope.

◎ A prayerless day. Get back on the wagon tomorrow. You'll feel better.

◎ The desire to check prayer off your to-do list. You're never through praying.

Focus Points...

Pray at all times and on every occasion in the power of the Holy Spirit. Stay alert and be persistent in your prayers for all Christians everywhere.
EPHESIANS 6:18 NLT

If you abide in Me, and My words abide in you, you will ask what you desire, and it shall be done for you.
JOHN 15:7 NKJV

When two or three of you are together because of me, you can be sure that I'll be there.
MATTHEW 18:20 MSG

When you pray, you should go into your room and close the door and pray to your Father who cannot be seen. Your Father can see what is done in secret, and he will reward you.
MATTHEW 6:6 NCV

Search me, O God, and know my heart; try me, and know my anxieties; and see if there is any wicked way in me, and lead me in the way everlasting.
PSALM 139:23–24 NKJV

The fewer the words, the better the prayer.

MARTIN LUTHER

Anything big enough to occupy our minds is big enough to hang a prayer on.

GEORGE MACDONALD

Prayer
The Prayer that God Answers

I call on you, O God, for you will answer me; give ear to me and hear my prayer.

PSALM 17:6 NIV

You might remember a country song from a few years ago: "Sometimes I thank God for unanswered prayers." It tells the story of a man, now happily married, who runs into an old girlfriend whom he once hoped to marry. He had prayed to marry her, but God didn't answer that prayer—or didn't answer yes, in any case. In the meantime, the man had gotten married to the woman he was truly meant for. So the sight of the woman he had once longed for wasn't wistful or sad, but rather an occasion to thank God for not giving him what he thought he wanted back then.

Sometimes is seems that God's answer to your prayers is always "No." You pour your heart out asking God for the things you truly desire. You remember those passages in the Bible that promise that God hears your prayers. "Whatever we ask we receive from Him, because we keep His commandments" (1 John 3:22 NKJV). "The effective, fervent prayer of a

238

righteous man avails much" (James 5:16 NKJV). But sometimes you don't get what you ask for, and you wonder what happened. Is God not listening? Are you not righteous enough? Does the Bible have it wrong about prayer?

If you had a daughter with a peanut allergy, you wouldn't give her a peanut butter sandwich no matter how much she seemed to want it or how many times she begged you for it. You thoughts are higher than hers, and you know what she needs more than she knows herself. It helps to realize that God always gives you what you would have asked for if you only knew what He knows. That's the prayer God answers.

God knows what you need more than you do. He even knows what you want more than you do, and that's what he's determined to give you, even if you're begging for something else. "'My thoughts are not your thoughts, nor are your ways My ways,' says the LORD. 'For as the heavens are higher than the earth, so are My ways higher than your ways, and My thoughts than your thoughts'" (Isaiah 55:8–9 NKJV). The time will come when you will know why some of your prayers have seemed to go unanswered. In the meantime, it is enough to rest in the God who calls you to cast your cares on Him.

Prayer
The Prayer that God Answers

What Matters Most...

- God's plan. It may not make sense now, but someday it will.

- Trust. You can leave the future to God.

- Your desires. They matter too, as long as they're submitted to Gods' will.

- Love. Your love for God, His love for you.

- Answered prayers. Don't forget about those times when God has unexpectedly given you what you asked for. Those memories strengthen you when it feels like God isn't answering your prayers.

What Doesn't Matter...

- Your frustrations. Pour them out to God, and trust Him.

- Your plans. Keep a very loose grip on your own plans for the future.

- Your tendency to bargain with God. Submission to God's will is the essence of prayer.

- Your idea of how things ought to be. God has it all under control.

- Your timing. Timing isn't your responsibility.

Focus Points...

Jesus used this story to teach his followers that they should always pray and never lose hope.
LUKE 18:1 NCV

Ask, and you will receive. Search, and you will find. Knock, and the door will be opened for you.
MATTHEW 7:7 GOD'S WORD

God's Spirit is right alongside helping us along. If we don't know how or what to pray, it doesn't matter. He does our praying in and for us, making prayer out of our wordless sighs, our aching groans.
ROMANS 8:26 MSG

You ask and do not receive, because you ask amiss, that you may spend it on your pleasures.
JAMES 4:3 NKJV

what really counts

Keep praying, but be thankful that God's answers are wiser than your prayers.

WILLIAM CULBERTSON

We forget that God sometimes has to say No. We pray to Him as our heavenly Father, and like wise human fathers, He often says, No, not from whim or caprice, but from wisdom and from love, and knowing what is best for us.

PETER MARSHALL

Prayer
Changing Your Mind

Confess your sins to each other and pray for each other so that you can live together whole and healed. The prayer of a person living right with God is something powerful to be reckoned with.

JAMES 5:16 MSG

When you pray, do you ever catch yourself making your case to God? Do you ever lay out the facts for God in a carefully constructed argument? "I need [fill in the blank] because [fill in three reasons]. If we can't work that out, I would be willing to settle for [fill in alternate blessing]." As if God needed anything explained to Him. As if human arguments might persuade Him. Can you really change God's mind through prayer? That's a mystery, but there's one thing you can know about how prayer works: It changes your mind. Earnest prayer lines up your will with the will of God.

Consider the prayer of Jesus in the Garden of Gethsemane, the night before He died. "O My Father, if it is possible, let this cup pass from Me" (Matthew 26:39 NKJV). He poured out His heart, getting real with His heavenly Father, asking to be spared the physical anguish of death on a cross. But the rest of that prayer revealed an even deeper desire:

"Nevertheless, not as I will, but as you will." He desired what any human being would desire in His situation: to be spared torture and death. But He had come to do the will of the Father. In His second prayer, you can sense a slight change in emphasis. Jesus seems to be accepting the fact that there is no other way: "O My Father, if this cup cannot pass away from Me unless I drink it, Your will be done" (Matthew 26:42 NKJV).

Yes, Jesus is fully God, but He was also fully human. That humanness had to come to terms with the fact that God could not change His plan. It was a prayer that made that acceptance possible. In the end, the purpose of that prayer was to change the human being who prayed it, not the God who heard it.

Prayer is a mysterious thing. The Bible makes it clear that God does not change His mind. But it also makes it clear that God listens to your prayers, that He delights to give His people what they want when they pray according to His will. Perhaps the mechanics of answered prayer are beyond human comprehension. But when you pray—when you seek God's will—you'd better be ready for the possibility that you're the one whose mind will get changed.

Prayer
Changing Your Mind

What Matters Most...

◎ Keeping open lines of communication between you and God.

◎ Being open to change. Prayer may or may not change your circumstances, but it will certainly change you.

◎ Drawing near to God. He will draw near to you.

◎ Righteousness. The earnest prayer of a righteous man is effective.

◎ Perseverance in prayer. Leave the results to God.

What Doesn't Matter...

◎ Your desire to make your case to God. God wants you to pour your heart out to Him, but there's little need to try to persuade God with human arguments.

◎ Having a "mountaintop experience" every time you pray. Sometimes prayer is hard work.

◎ Understanding how prayer works. In many regards prayer is just a mystery.

◎ Your stubbornness. Prayer changes you. You might as well be ready for it.

◎ Your fears. God always has your best interests at heart.

Focus Points...

Take delight in the LORD, and he will give you the desires of your heart.
PSALM 37:4 NRSV

The prayer offered in faith will make the sick person well; the Lord will raise him up.
JAMES 5:15 NIV

I pray for these followers, but I am also praying for all those who will believe in me because of their teaching.
JOHN 17:20 NCV

The sacrifice of the wicked is an abomination to the LORD, but the prayer of the upright is His delight.
PROVERBS 15:8 NKJV

The Lord watches over the righteous and listens to their prayers; but he opposes those who do evil.
1 PETER 3:12 GNT

what really counts

The one concern of the devil is to keep Christians from praying ... He laughs at our toil, mocks at our wisdom, but trembles when we pray.

SAMUEL CHADWICK

Never doubt in the dark what God has told you in the light.

V. RAYMOND EDMAN

What Matters Most to Me About
Prayer

Prayer is really a matter of marshalling all the resources that are available to you as a son of God. Prayer may seem completely natural to you. You can't imagine going a day without chatting with your heavenly father. Or it could be a chore you've been avoiding. Write down some thoughts here.

◎ *Read the Lord's prayer in Matthew 6:9-13. You've probably had it memorized for years, but is there anything you can apply to your own prayer life today?*

_____

_____

_____

_____

_____

_____

_____

_____

_____

◎ *Why do you think Jesus often went off alone to pray to God?*

_____

_____

_____

_____

_____

_____

what
really
counts

Have you received an answer to a prayer lately? Write down your experience here.

_____

_____

_____

_____

_____

_____

_____

_____

_____

Have you been getting a steady no for any of your prayers? Write a prayer to God in which you tell him how you feel about that. You can be honest; God knows your heart anyway.

_____

_____

_____

_____

_____

_____

_____

_____

_____

_____

To be a Christian without prayer is no more possible than to be alive without breathing.

MARTIN LUTHER

SIN

An Introduction

> All have sinned and fall short of the glory of God.
> ROMANS 3:23 NKJV

what really counts

Think about the difference between bacteria and cancer. Bacteria cells have a life of their own. They invade your body from the outside, then they grow and multiply, making you sick by attacking your good cells. Cancer is different. Though people speak of cancer cells, it's something of a misnomer. A cancerous cell doesn't have a life of its own in the same way a virus or a bacterium does. Cancer exists only as a corruption of normal cells that are already in a person's body. It doesn't invade from the outside; it works from the inside out.

Sin is a cancer, not a bacteria. It works from the inside out, not from the outside in. More to the point, it exists only as a corruption of the good. Take sexual

248

sin, for example. The desire for sexual union is a God-given desire. Every sexual sin, no matter how depraved, is a corruption of that desire. In the same way, greed is a corruption of the God-given impulse to provide for yourself and your family. Sloth is a corruption of the God-designed need for rest. That's not to say that sin is a minor matter. It's more of a killer than cancer has ever been.

The good news is that the Great Physician is ready to heal you of the sin that is wasting your spiritual life away. No sin goes so deep that God can't reach in and heal it. Your case doesn't have to be terminal.

> It is not only that sin consists in doing evil, but also in not doing the good that we know.
> H. A. IRONSIDE

Sin
Turning Back

In those days John the Baptist came, preaching in the Wilderness of Judea and saying, "Repent, because the kingdom of heaven has come near!"

MATTHEW 3:1–2 HCSB

what really counts

The wild man in goatskins, the one called John the Baptist, preached his usual refrain: "Repent, for the kingdom of God is at hand!" it was a pretty simple message: Get a new way of thinking because a new way of living, a new way of relating to God has come in the person of Jesus Christ. He wasn't preaching to pagans. He was preaching mostly to good Jews, people who lived good lives and thought they had their spiritual lives in order. But they needed a new way of thinking no less than the most heathen of their neighbors.

We usually think of repentance as relating to actions: You stop doing bad things and start doing good things. But that change in behavior is actually the result of repentance. It's not repentance itself. Repentance is a change of mind. In the Greek, the word translated *repent* literally means "to think again," or perhaps it's better to say, "to rethink." That change of inner state inevitably results in new outward actions.

Repentance is a turning away from sin and—more importantly—a turning toward the things of God. The nineteenth-century Scottish preacher Thomas Chalmers preached a famous sermon on "the expulsive power of a new affection." Those are big words, but the gist of Chalmers' sermon is relatively simple. By nature you love to sin. That's the old affection. The only way to overcome that natural love of sin is to replace it with a love for God. That's the "new affection" that expels the old. That's the nature of true repentance. Chalmers wouldn't have had much patience for the old "Just Say No" anti-drug campaign. You can't "just say no." You have to say yes to something. If you haven't said yes to God, you haven't yet repented of anything. You have only turned from one kind of sin to a new kind, but when you have said yes to God, you can be sure he'll say yes to you.

The Gospel is the ultimate bad news-good news scenario. The bad news is that you are a sinner. You were born that way, sinful at your very root, but the good news overwhelms the bad news: God forgives and welcomes repentant sinners. No sin is beyond God's power to redeem. As He invades a sinner's heart, He routs the sin that would destroy your soul.

Sin
Turning Back

What Matters Most...

◎ Facing the fact of your nature. It's the first step in overcoming sin.

◎ Turning away from your sin. It need not have a hold on you any longer.

◎ Turning toward God. You have to say yes to God before you can truly say no to sin.

◎ Receiving God's forgiveness. When you repent, He separates you and your sin as far as the east is from the west.

◎ Moving on. You have a new life, a new self in Christ.

What **Doesn't** Matter...

◎ The depth of your past sin. God's grace goes deeper.

◎ Your feelings of guilt. If you are in Christ, you are a new creature.

◎ Sin's continued guerilla attacks. They matter, but not as much as the love of God, which will defeat them.

◎ Feelings of aloneness. God is at your side—not to mention your fellow believers.

◎ Feelings of weakness. God is strong in you.

Focus Points...

God is being patient with you. He does not want anyone to be lost, but he wants all people to change their hearts and lives.
2 PETER 3:9 NCV

Forget about what's happened; don't keep going over old history. Be alert, be present. I'm about to do something brand-new. It's bursting out! Don't you see it? There it is! I'm making a road through the desert, rivers in the badlands.
ISAIAH 43:18–19 MSG

Count on it—there's more joy in heaven over one sinner's rescued life than over ninety-nine good people in no need of rescue.
LUKE 15:7 MSG

what really counts

If we confess our sins, he will forgive our sins, because we can trust God to do what is right. He will cleanse us from all the wrongs we have done.
1 JOHN 1:9 NCV

God has cast our confessed sins into the depths of the sea, and He's even put a "No Fishing" sign over the spot.
DWIGHT MOODY

Either sin is with you, lying on your shoulders, or it is lying on Christ, the Lamb of God.
MARTIN LUTHER

Sin
Fighting Back

I confessed my sins to you; I did not conceal my wrongdoings. I decided to confess them to you, and you forgave all my sins.

PSALM 32:5 GNT

Have you ever been overcome by temptation? The opportunity to sin presents itself, and it looks so good. It seems so much more interesting and exotic than the day-to-day life you lead that you really don't have a choice. How could you avoid it? You have to sin. Actually you haven't ever been "overcome" by temptation. No doubt you've yielded to temptation. You have chosen to sin rather than doing the right thing. But you always have a choice; that's what makes it a temptation. "The only temptation that has come to you is that which everyone has. But you can trust God, who will not permit you to be tempted more than you can stand. But when you are tempted, he will also give you a way to escape so that you will be able to stand it" (1 Corinthians 10:13 NCV).

God always provides a way out. Often it's a door. Often escaping temptation is as easy as leaving the place where the temptation occurs. "Lead us not into temptation." You've

254

uttered those words countless times. But how often do men knowingly lead themselves into temptation? If they're honest with themselves, people usually know where they're going to be tempted to the same old sins. A man who puts himself in that situation makes a mockery of the request he recites on Sunday morning: "Lead us not into temptation." The truth is, he's already sinned by choosing to go there. At that point, the question is whether or not he's going to sin again when the expected temptation presents itself.

Of course, there are situations where temptation just sneaks up on you. Those are the situations for which you pray for God's protection and guidance. He is faithful to guard you when you seek His help. Being tempted is not a sin. It's a test, and like any other test, it's good is you pass, bad if you fail.

You'll never be perfect this side of heaven. Even when you're in Christ, you're still wrestling with the old you. Think about how many times you have chosen to sin—to yield to temptation—just in the last two days. Each of those sins could have been avoided. You could have been that much closer to perfection. When you're presented with a temptation, the manly thing is to fight back. God always provides a way out.

Sin
Fighting Back

What Matters Most...

◎ The way out. God always provides one when you're tempted.

◎ The way up. Overcoming temptation draws you nearer to God and gives you reason to celebrate.

◎ A clear head. Your feelings can get away from you when you're tempted. You need a clear head to remember that there's always a way out—and that it's always the right way.

◎ Integrity. Nobody's looking? God will know. So will you.

◎ God's promises. Don't let temptation make you forget what God promises to those who overcome.

What **Doesn't** Matter...

◎ Your excuses. Take responsibility for your own integrity.

◎ Your weakness. There's a way out, even when you aren't feeling so strong.

◎ The seeming inescapability of temptation. You can escape.

◎ The feeling that you've been tainted by temptations you didn't seek out. A temptation is a test; it can't taint you unless you yield to it.

◎ The feeling that it's too late to escape a temptation. It's never too late to do the right thing.

Focus Points...

When they arrived at the place, he said, "Pray that you don't give in to temptation."
LUKE 22:40 MSG

Give yourselves completely to God. Stand against the devil, and the devil will run from you.
JAMES 4:7 NCV

No temptation has overtaken you except such as is common to man; but God is faithful, who will not allow you to be tempted beyond what you are able, but with the temptation will also make the way of escape, that you may be able to bear it.
1 CORINTHIANS 10:13 NKJV

Guide my steps as you promised; don't let any sin control me.
PSALM 119:133 NCV

**what
really
counts**

Though we cannot eliminate temptation to sin, we are not left without redemptive resources. God is on our side, Jesus is advocating for us, and the Holy Spirit is making us aware of our weaknesses.

DAVID MCKENNA

The Christian life is not difficult; it is impossible. It is a supernatural life. When I try, I fail, but when I trust, God succeeds.
HOWARD HENDRICKS

What Matters Most to Me About
Sin

It's a fact. Everybody is a sinner by nature, but another fact overwhelms that one: God forgives those who confess their sin and turn from it.

◎ *Name two or three areas in your life that you are struggling with. Can you think of Scriptures that clearly label these difficult spots as sin?*

_____

_____

_____

_____

_____

_____

_____

_____

◎ *Write down a prayer here, confessing these sins to God as He asks you to in 1 John 1:9.*

_____

_____

_____

_____

_____

_____

_____

what
really
counts

◎ *Remember a sin you have repented of. How has your thinking about that sin changed?*

_____

_____

_____

_____

_____

_____

_____

_____

_____

◎ *Consider an area in which you have been known to lead yourself into temptation. What are some specific ways you can keep yourself out of that situation?*

_____

_____

_____

_____

_____

_____

_____

_____

_____

The battle for sin is won or lost in your mind.
Whatever gets your attention will get you.
RICK WARREN

FAMILY AND RELATIONSHIPS
An Introduction

> Just as a father has compassion on his children, so the LORD has compassion on those who fear Him.
>
> PSALM 103:13 NASB

what really counts

Jesus spoke of the kingdom of God growing and expanding like a mustard plant, starting out as a tiny seed and then burgeoning into a plant that's big enough for birds to perch in. What do you picture when you think of the kingdom of God growing and expanding? Maybe you picture a Billy Graham crusade with hundreds of people streaming down stadium steps to pray the Sinner's Prayer and receive Christ. Perhaps you think of the tireless efforts of pastors preaching the Gospel every week from pulpits across the world. Both are hugely important means by which God grows His kingdom. But don't forget the quieter but equally powerful work of Christian families pointing their little ones toward Christ. Here is the power of the Gospel; here is church growth in its purest form.

Of the three great social institutions—Church, government, and family—family is the most ancient and also the most basic. Without functioning families, both government and churches find it very difficult to carry out their appointed missions. That's why it's such a disaster when fathers abdicate their responsibility to lead their families—some by leaving, some by being present only in body.

If you are a husband and father, you have a sacred duty to teach your family what God is like and to point them toward the Cross. That's not a job for you to delegate to a preacher or a Sunday school teacher. Are you up to the challenge?

> You may not be able to leave your children a great inheritance, but day by day, you may be weaving coats for them which they will wear for all eternity.
>
> THEODORE L. CUYLER

Family and Relationships
Servant Leadership

> Even I, the Son of Man, came here not to be served but to serve others, and to give my life as a ransom for many.
>
> MATTHEW 20:28 NLT

what really counts

During the American Revolution, a small group of American soldiers was struggling to build a redoubt. Their commander was shouting orders but hadn't lifted a finger to help them finish the job. A second officer, unknown to the commander and dressed in civilian clothes, came by on horseback and, seeing the men hard at work, asked the commander why he wasn't helping. "Sir, I am a corporal!" the man answered, his dignity a little offended at the suggestion that he should have to help with such lowly work as building a redoubt. So the stranger dismounted and pitched in with the privates. When the work was done, the stranger got back on his horse. "Mr. Corporal," he said, "next time you have a job like this and not enough men to do it, go to your commander-in-chief, and I will come and help you again." It was only then that the corporal recognized the strange officer. He was George Washington.

True leadership is servant leadership. His last night on earth, Jesus stooped down and washed His disciples' feet—a job fit only for the lowest of servants. "Kings like to throw their weight around," he explained, "and people in authority like to give themselves fancy titles. It's not going to be that way with you. Let the senior among you become like the junior; let the leader act the part of the servant" (Luke 22:25–26 MSG).

If you want your family—or anybody else—to follow your leadership gladly, you have to show them that you have their best interests at heart. If you demonstrate to them that you're going to use your leadership role to lead them toward what's best for them, and not just to get more of what you want, they'll be happy to follow. One way you do that is by serving—by lightening your wife's load around the house, by laying aside your agenda now and then and giving your full attention to your kids, by showing your subordinates at work that you value them as people and not merely as "human resources."

Servant leadership runs counter to the way the world views power and leadership. But that's not surprising coming from the One who promised that the first would be last and the last first. Do you want to be exalted? Then get down off your horse and get to work.

Family and Relationships
Servant Leadership

What Matters Most...

- ◎ Your role as leader. God has given you authority in the home.

- ◎ Your role as servant. Even as a leader, you are here to serve, not to be served.

- ◎ The well-being of your family. Convince them that you put their well-being first, and they'll follow your lead.

- ◎ Christ's example. His leadership style is your model.

- ◎ The dignity of service. You're showing your family what God looks like.

What **Doesn't** Matter...

- ◎ The world's view of power and authority. God's view runs counter.

- ◎ The urge to use others instead of serving them. Squelch it.

- ◎ The tendency to equate service with weakness. There was nothing weak about Jesus.

- ◎ Your ego. Servant leadership will do wonders for your self-image.

- ◎ Your laziness. You can fulfill your responsibilities in your home.

Focus Points...

Serve wholeheartedly, as if you were serving the Lord, not men.
EPHESIANS 6:7 NIV

We who are strong ought to bear the weaknesses of those without strength and not just please ourselves.
ROMANS 15:1 NASB

I am free and belong to no one. But I make myself a slave to all people to win as many as I can.
1 CORINTHIANS 9:19 NCV

Let each of you look out not only for his own interests, but also for the interests of others.
PHILIPPIANS 2:4 NKJV

what really counts

We, though, are going to love—love and be loved. First we were loved, now we love. He loved us first.
1 JOHN 4:19 MSG

The image of George Washington kneeling in prayer at Valley Forge says something about the method of all leadership—humble, modest service.

GEORGE SWEETING

A Christian man is the most free lord of all, and subject to none; a Christian man is the most dutiful servant of all, and subject to everyone.

MARTIN LUTHER

Family and Relationships
Don't Exasperate

> Fathers, do not exasperate your children; instead, bring them up in the training and instruction of the Lord.
>
> EPHESIANS 6:4 NIV

If you have children, you know how exasperating they can be. They dawdle. They spill things. They don't follow instructions. But you can read the Bible from cover to cover, and you won't find a verse that reads, "Children, don't exasperate your fathers." You might as well look for a verse that reads, "Dogs, don't shed," or "Fish, don't swim." Children can't help but be exasperating. They're little. They're uncoordinated. They're still learning what's expected of them. What you will find in the Bible, however, is a verse that reads, "Fathers, do not exasperate your children" (Colossians 3:21 NASB).

Why is that? Why are fathers singled out that way when everybody else in the family is more likely to exasperate the father than the other way around? It's because the stakes are so high when a father exasperates his child. If your son slams the screen door for the hundredth time, it's aggravating, but it's not going to damage your soul. On the other hand, a father who isn't careful with his children's feelings can do lasting harm. Consider the rest of the verse from Colossians 3:21—"Fathers, do not exasperate your children, that they may not lose heart." It's a pitiful thing to think about—your own child losing heart because of the way you treat them.

It's a question of power. You have it, your kids don't. They don't really have any recourse if your edicts are arbitrary or unjust. If you yell at them, they can't really yell back. If you ignore them, they may not have any way of getting your attention besides annoying you and bringing more trouble on themselves. When you frustrate your children, it often goes beyond mere annoyance. It may be more like the rage of powerlessness. That's not good for a child's spirit. Your children's souls are yours to nurture. It falls to you, therefore, to use your authority over them gently, fairly, mercifully. It falls to you to show them what their heavenly Father looks like.

The people who are the closest to you are the easiest to exasperate. But when you, the father of the house, exasperate your family, you run the risk of causing them to lose heart. That's a grave risk. You were put in authority over your family not to be served, but to serve—to usher your family into the kingdom of God. So handle your loved ones with care.

Family and Relationships
Don't Exasperate

What Matters Most...

⊙ The souls of your family. It's your job and your joy to nurture them.

⊙ Your children's love for you. A kind word builds them up.

⊙ Your authority in the home. Use it wisely, deliberately for the good of your family.

⊙ God's mercy toward you. Pass it on to your family. Be loving and forgiving.

⊙ God's commands to fathers. He holds you responsible.

What Doesn't Matter...

⊙ Your desire for peace and quiet around the house. That may not be where your family is right now.

⊙ The natural tendency to lord it over your children. Resist it.

⊙ Old habits. Christ came to make new men, with new habits.

⊙ Your own memories of a less than perfect father. It is time to break a cycle.

⊙ A sense of fatherly entitlement. Your family is a gift from God.

Focus Points...

He will turn the hearts of the fathers to the children, and the hearts of the children to their fathers.
MALACHI 4:6 NKJV

My son, keep your father's commands and do not forsake your mother's teaching. Bind them upon your heart forever.
PROVERBS 6:20–21 NIV

Honor your father and mother. Then you will live a long, full life in the land the LORD your God will give you.
EXODUS 20:12 NLT

Correction and punishment make children wise, but those left alone will disgrace their mother.
PROVERBS 29:15 NCV

what really counts

Be kind and loving to each other, and forgive each other just as God forgave you in Christ.
EPHESIANS 4:32 NCV

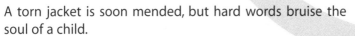

A torn jacket is soon mended, but hard words bruise the soul of a child.

HENRY WADSWORTH LONGFELLOW

When you teach your son, you teach your son's son.

THE TALMUD

What Matters Most to Me About
Family and Relationships

Being godly means taking the initiative in your relationships so that you can serve others and love them well. With your authority comes awesome responsibility.

◎ *Do you exasperate those who are closest to you? What can you do to start building those people back up?*

_____
_____
_____
_____
_____
_____
_____
_____

what
really
counts

◎ *How can you demonstrate to your loved ones that you have their best interests at heart?*

_____
_____
_____
_____
_____
_____
_____

◎ *Write about a time someone has refused to follow your leadership.*
What did you learn from that situation?

_____

_____

_____

_____

_____

_____

_____

_____

_____

◎ *What are your deepest hopes for your family? Are those hopes in*
line with the things that matter most according to the Bible?

_____

_____

_____

_____

_____

_____

_____

_____

_____

One father is more than a hundred
schoolmasters.

GEORGE HERBERT

SIGNIFICANCE

An Introduction

> Sometimes our humble hearts can help us more than our proud minds.
>
> 1 CORINTHIANS 8:2 MSG

what really counts

Do you ever have mountaintop experiences, when life seems to be firing on all cylinders and everything seems to make sense? You feel close to God, you feel a renewed zeal to love others, and the truths of the Scriptures seem very true in your life. Such experiences are great when you can get them. But Oswald Chambers had something interesting to say about the mountaintop: "We are not made for the mountains, for the sunrises, or for the other beautiful attractions of life: those are simply intended to be moments of inspiration. We are made for the valley and for the ordinary things."

The ordinary things. That's life—a sequence of ordinary moments punctuated by the occasional moment of extraordinariness. Yet life is so much more than that too, for those moments that seem so ordinary are actually pregnant with eternal meaning. Every conversation you have, no matter how mundane, is a conversation with an immortal. Every action you perform is performed under the eye of the Maker of heaven and earth, who watches to see what you will make of it. The truth is, if you can't find significance in the everyday, you can't find it anywhere.

Your life has significance because you are made in the image of God. That's as true for you as it is for the most brilliant scientist, the most famous celebrity, the most generous philanthropist. Every day you get a little closer to perfect conformity with the image of God. That's real significance.

> When you reach the mountaintop, you're only halfway.
>
> MOUNTAIN CLIMBERS' PROVERB

Significance
Everyday Spirituality

The earth is the Lord's, and all its fullness, the world and those who dwell therein.

PSALM 24:1 NKJV

what really counts

The earth is the Lord's, and all its fullness. Ponder that for a while. Rocks, trees, oceans, rivers—all are God's. Your job, your family, your hobbies; governments, the entertainment industry, the educational system—those things belong to God too. They are often misused by human beings, but still they belong to God. Sometimes people, including Christians, put up false barriers between the spiritual life and the rest of life, as if the Church belonged to God and everything else belonged to somebody else. But God makes it clear: It all belongs to Him.

What does it mean to be in the world and yet to be truly spiritual? It means you see the spiritual significance of everything you encounter. You view the things of earth as raw materials for building the kingdom of God. You look at every aspect of your life and ask, "How might I glorify God in this?" Sometimes that means rejecting things that war against God's kingdom. You can't steal or cheat or drive drunk for God's glory. But there's a lot more to spirituality than sitting in judgment of the world. At its root, spirituality is about transforming your whole life into something that pleases God, using the good gifts He has given you to advance His kingdom: your money, your health, your talents, your influence, your talents, your relationships.

It's true that the Bible describes Christians as aliens and strangers in the world (see 1 Peter 2:11). Christians are called not to get too comfortable with the things of the world. But renouncing your citizenship in the world isn't the point so much as claiming your citizenship in heaven. Someday you'll reside there, where your citizenship truly lies, but in the meantime you're part of the advance party, helping to lay the groundwork for the day when it will be obvious to everyone that God reigns in heaven and earth.

In the book of Revelation, the angel announces, "The kingdoms of this world have become the kingdoms of our Lord" (Revelation 11:15 NKJV). That's the work God is doing: not discarding or rejecting a broken world, but reclaiming it as His own. You have a role to play in that—a role you can't perform if you've put up a false barrier between your spiritual life and the rest of life. Everything you do, no matter how mundane it seems, has spiritual significance. The trick is learning to see it.

Significance
Everyday Spirituality

What Matters Most...

◎ Seeing that all things belong to God. The earth is the Lord's, and all that is in it.

◎ A changed life. You can please God in everything you do.

◎ The kingdom of God. He is always at work.

◎ Love. It's your motivation for all right conduct in the world.

◎ Discernment. Pray to know what glorifies God and what doesn't.

What Doesn't Matter...

◎ The sacred/secular divide. Everything is God's. All the world belongs to God.

◎ Your earthly citizenship. Your true citizenship is in heaven.

◎ Excitement. Some days are more exciting than others, but all of them are a gift from God.

◎ The seeming meaninglessness of the world. God imbues everything with meaning.

◎ Your self-importance. Your importance comes from God. You are important because of God.

Focus Points…

Don't shuffle along, eyes to the ground, absorbed with the things right in front of you. Look up, and be alert to what is going on around Christ—that's where the action is. See things from his perspective.
COLOSSIANS 3:2 MSG

Be careful how you live. Don't live like ignorant people, but like wise people.
EPHESIANS 5:15 GNT

I can do everything through Christ who strengthens me.
PHILIPPIANS 4:13 GOD'S WORD

Turn my eyes away from worthless things. Give me a new life in your ways.
PSALM 119:37 GOD'S WORD

what really counts

Sometimes when I consider what tremendous consequences come from little things, I am tempted to think there are no little things.

BRUCE BARTON

There's some task which the God of all the universe … has for you to do, and which will remain undone and incomplete until by faith and obedience you step into the will of God.

ALAN REDPATH

277

Significance
Upward, Outward, Inward

> I keep trying to reach the goal and get the prize for which God called me through Christ to the life above.
> PHILIPPIANS 3:14 NCV

what really counts

If someone were to hold up a screwdriver and ask "What is this?" how would you answer? You could, of course, answer, "It's a six-inch rod of steel, one end of which is embedded in hard plastic, the other end of which is flattened." That would be an accurate description of a screwdriver, but it wouldn't be very helpful. Really, there's no good way to define a screwdriver without talking about what it's made for, how it relates to other things. You would probably explain how the flat end is for driving screws. You might explain that the plastic end is a handle, designed to be held and turned by the human hand.

How about the question, "What are you?" You're a carbon-based life form, a member of the species *homo sapiens,* but that doesn't really answer the question. Because the question, really, is what were you made for? What is your relationship to others? You might look deep inside yourself to find an answer; that would be a good place to start. Your tal-

278

ents, your hopes, your likes and dislikes, your values—all those things distinguish you from other people and define who you are.

But looking inside won't give you the full picture of who you are. You also have to look upward, to the God who created you in order to have a relationship with you. Your significance derives from the fact that you were made in His image, made to reflect that image back to Him and out to the world around you. Which brings up the third direction to look for significance: outward. Look inward to yourself, look upward to God, and look outward to the people around you. They define you too. You may be somebody's husband, somebody's father, somebody's son, somebody's employee, somebody's boss. There are a lot of people who depend on you. As you look out into the world, you see what gives you significance: loving others, showing them what God is like, being part of something bigger than yourself.

It's been said that the unexamined life is not worth living. That's true enough. Yet that call to self-examination doesn't justify a life dominated by introspection. Real significance, as Jesus said, comes from loving God with all your heart, soul, and mind, and loving others as yourself. If you're looking for significance, look inward, look upward, and look outward.

Significance
Upward, Outward, Inward

What Matters Most...

- ◎ Looking upward to God. He is before all things, and in Him all things hold together.

- ◎ Looking outward to the people around you. Your relationships help define who you are.

- ◎ Looking for ways to help others. You have so much to offer to others.

- ◎ Looking for answers from God's Word. It will make you a wise person.

- ◎ Looking for success in God's eyes. His opinion is the one that ultimately matters.

What Doesn't Matter...

- ◎ Labels. They just don't matter. When you're looking outward, labels can obscure your view.

- ◎ Outside appearances. God doesn't care how people look on the outside; it's character that matters most.

- ◎ Earthly achievements. God has a whole other definition of success and significance.

- ◎ Others' opinions of you. Only one person matters, and that is Jesus Christ. Are you living your life to please Him?

- ◎ Self-focus. Too much self can drain your time and energy from serving others.

Focus Points...

As you therefore have received Christ Jesus the Lord, so walk in Him, rooted and built up in Him and esablished in the faith, as you have been taught, abounding in it with thanksgiving.

COLOSSIANS 2:6–7 NKJV

All of God lives in Christ fully (even when Christ was on earth), and you have a full and true life in Christ, who is ruler over all rulers and powers.

COLOSSIANS 2:9–10 NCV

Be kindly affectionate to one another with brotherly love, in honor giving preference to one another.

ROMANS 12:10 NKJV

I am in prison because I belong to the Lord. God chose you to be his people, so I urge you now to live the life to which God called you.

EPHESIANS 4:1 NCV

what
really
counts

A Christian should always remember that the value of his good works is not based on their number and excellence, but on the love of God which prompts him to do these things.

SAINT JOHN OF THE CROSS

An accurate understanding of God's truth is the first step toward discovering our significance and worth.

ROBERT S. MCGEE

What Matters Most to Me About
Significance

A proper self-image isn't just about how you view yourself, but also how God views you. You have to consider both. In other words, try to think of yourself the same way God thinks of you.

◎ *Who are some people you respect? What is it about these people that you value?*

_____

_____

_____

_____

_____

_____

what
really
counts

_____

_____

◎ *Where do you find your self-worth? Are there any Bible verses that you feel give you significance?*

_____

_____

_____

_____

_____

_____

_____

_____

⊙ *How does it change your view of yourself if you realize you are a son of God? What kinds of blessings are bestowed upon children of royalty?*

_____

_____

_____

_____

_____

_____

_____

_____

_____

⊙ *Write down some things you can do this week to show others you value them more than yourself.*

_____

_____

_____

_____

_____

_____

_____

_____

_____

_____

Resolution One: I will live for God. Resolution Two: If no one else does, I still will.

JONATHAN EDWARDS

WORK AND CAREER
An Introduction

> Don't you remember the rule we had when we lived with you? "If you don't work, you don't eat."
> 2 THESSALONIANS 3:10 MSG

what really counts

When Adam and Eve were still in the Garden of Eden, before they had ever sinned, God gave them work to do. They had no need of money. They could pluck their food from almost any tree or bush. They had no clothing budget. They weren't saving for their kids' braces or college tuition. Yet they had work to do. "The LORD God took the man and put him in the garden of Eden to tend and keep it" (Genesis 2:15 NKJV). Imagine that: It was a perfect world, but God put Adam and Eve to work.

That truth tells you at least one thing about the nature of work: It's not merely an inconvenience or an unfortunate fact of adult life. It's not even a necessary evil resulting from human sin. It's an integral part of what God had always intended human beings to be. It's one of the things you were put here for. Or to put it another way, work is one of the most important ways you live out God's plan for you.

It pleases God when you do your work acknowledging that He—and not your earthly boss—is the one you're really working for. But like any of God's gifts, work can be corrupted and abused. It can become an idol, displacing God on the throne of your heart. The trick is to think highly of the work God has entrusted you with, but not too highly.

> We must not grow weary of doing little things for the love of God, who looks not on the great size of the work, but on the love in it.
>
> BROTHER LAWRENCE

Work and Career
What's Your Calling?

> Let the beauty of the LORD our God be upon
> us, and establish the work of our hands for
> us; yes, establish the work of our hands.
>
> PSALM 90:17 NKJV

**what
really
counts**

Do you view your work as a vocation? The word *vocation* literally means "calling." You're called to some work, and as you do that work, you have an opportunity to glorify God and to love and serve your neighbor. To think of your work as a calling is to view yourself as a steward of the work God has given you to do—not the master or owner of your career, but a servant entrusted with a vitally important job. As you accept your work and do it joyfully, you fulfill one of God's most important purposes for your life. By bringing your talents to bear in the workplace, you are contributing to the well-being of your fellow citizens and acknowledging the goodness of the God who gave you the privilege of putting His blessings into use. It is not just a responsibility, but also a deep joy.

The Puritan William Perkins wrote, "The main end of our lives is to serve God in the serving of men . . . in the works of our callings." The goal of the Christian life, according to

Perkins, is not prayer, not contemplation or the singing of hymns, but a career submitted to serving God and man. Richard Steele, another Puritan, said that the one place "where you may most confidently expect the presence and blessing of God" was not in the church building, but in the workshop.

It may seem surprising that the Puritans, so famous for their deep spirituality, would exalt the earthly pursuit of work so highly. But they understood that if prayer and worship were one side of a coin, work was the other. Your work is one of the most important ways that your prayers and worship make themselves felt in the larger world. Conversely, your work will be meaningless if it's not empowered by prayer and worship. This realization is how work becomes more than a chore or a burden. This is what makes work joyful.

Your job is no less sacred than your pastor's. Everybody knows that a minister's job is to glorify God and to serve Him by loving and serving others. You're called to the same work. Do you view your work as a calling? If you don't, or if you can't, you won't find much happiness in it. But if you do, you can experience the joy and peace of fulfilling God's purpose for your life.

Work and Career
What's Your Calling?

What Matters Most...

- Finding your calling. That's the work that satisfies.

- Knowing who your real Boss is. God puts your tasks before you.

- Stewardship. Your vocation is given to you in trust.

- The joy of meaningful work. Work is always meaningful when you do everything as for the Lord.

- God's glory and the good of your neighbors. That's why you work.

What Doesn't Matter...

- Meniality. There are no menial tasks if you do your work with a view to glorifying God and serving others.

- Other people's opinions. You're working to please God.

- Shortcuts. The work that glorifies God is honest and conscientious.

- Making lots of money. There's more to work than your paycheck.

- Office politics. Your validation comes from God, not from an office pecking order.

Focus Points...

Jesus said, "My food is to do what the One who sent me wants me to do and to finish his work."
JOHN 4:34 NCV

Let him who stole steal no longer, but rather let him labor, working with his hands what is good, that he may have something to give him who has need.
EPHESIANS 4:28 NKJV

Dear friends, as you always obeyed me when I was with you, it is even more important that you obey me now while I am away from you. Keep on working with fear and trembling to complete your salvation.
PHILIPPIANS 2:12 GNT

what
really
counts

Whatever you do, do it heartily, as to the Lord and not to men.
COLOSSIANS 3:23 NKJV

Whoever compels you to go one mile, go with him two.
MATTHEW 5:41 NKJV

Work well done rises like a hymn of praise to God.
WILLIAM BARCLAY

Laziness may appear attractive, but work gives satisfaction.
ANNE FRANK

Work and Career
Who You Are, What You Do

It is God who works in you both to
will and to do for His good pleasure.
PHILIPPIANS 2:13 NKJV

what
really
counts

Once before an important trial, Chief Justice Louis
Brandeis went ahead and took a scheduled vacation. When
someone criticized him for what they viewed as putting
leisure before work, the judge replied, "I find I can do a year's
work in eleven months, but not in twelve." Sometimes giving
your all at work requires that you not give all to your work.
Your career is a vitally important part of life, but it isn't your
whole life. When work eats up all rest and leisure and keeps
you from tending to the other things that matter most in your
life, you are no longer serving God through your work.
Ironically, you can't do your best work.

Even if you are blessed to be working at your true vocation, there's more to life than your career. You have many
vocations—many roles you're called to fulfill. Husband and
father. Son to aging parents. Coach. Mentor. Church member.
Friend. You have a calling in every aspect of your life. Those

multiple callings add up to who you are. If your commitment to your career has pushed out even one of those callings, you aren't being everything God means for you to be. You aren't being yourself.

One of the big problems you face is the fact that you live in a society that defines men by what they do for a living. The measure of a man in this culture is his job title, his salary, the number of underlings he can boss around, the trappings of material success. How about you? Are you up when things are going well at work, and down when they aren't? To a certain degree that's unavoidable. Of course work affects your mood; it's part of who you are. But give yourself this test: Does your family life go up and down with your work life? Do your friendships?

What you do for a living isn't the same thing as who you are. Every man wants to succeed in his career. It is right to throw your whole self into your work. But bear in mind that in order to have a whole self to throw into your work, you have to answer all of your callings—and throw yourself into those callings too. At work and elsewhere, you can be everything God wants you to be.

Work and Career
Who You Are, What You Do

What Matters Most...

◎ Perspective. Work is important, but not the most important thing in the world.

◎ Balance. You have many callings and must tend to all of them.

◎ Commitment. Throw your whole self into all of your callings.

◎ Rest. You are a man, not a machine, and God made you to rest as well as to work.

◎ A Godward view. When your nose is to the grindstone, it takes a conscious effort to look up to God.

What **Doesn't** Matter...

◎ Pressure to look like the busiest person in the office. The busiest person in the office is rarely the best-balanced.

◎ Pressure to make more money. God knows what you need, and He always provides.

◎ Your job title. The real question is, are you answering all your callings?

◎ A career's tendency to suck up all your available time and energy. Resist. Live your whole life.

◎ Society's tendency to equate a man with his job. Your selfhood derives from God's love for you, and that doesn't depend on your job title.

Focus Points...

Do all you can to live a peaceful life. Take care of your own business, and do your own work as we have already told you.
1 THESSALONIANS 4:11 NCV

Don't waste your energy striving for perishable food like that. Work for the food that sticks with you, food that nourishes your lasting life, food the Son of Man provides.
JOHN 6:27 MSG

God has made us what we are. In Christ Jesus, God made us to do good works, which God planned in advance for us to live our lives doing.
EPHESIANS 2:10 NCV

In the same way, you should be a light for other people. Live so that they will see the good things you do and will praise your Father in heaven.
MATTHEW 5:16 NCV

what really counts

The place God calls you to is where your deep gladness and the world's deep hunger meet.

FREDERICK BUECHNER

Everybody wants to save the earth; nobody wants to help Mom do the dishes.

P. J. O'ROURKE

What Matters Most to Me About
Work and Career

A godly attitude toward work is a feat of balance. You have to value work as a gift from God, and yet not value it so much that it becomes an idol. Here are some questions to help you start sorting it all out.

◎ *What do your really expect to get out of work? Is that a realistic expectation? Is it a godly expectation?*

_____

_____

_____

_____

_____

_____

_____

◎ *What makes you get out of bed and go to work every morning?*

_____

_____

_____

_____

_____

_____

_____

what
really
counts

◎ *What are new ways you can love and serve your coworkers? How about your clients or customers?*

_____

_____

_____

_____

_____

_____

_____

_____

_____

◎ *Do you feel that you're working at your true vocation? Why or why not?*

_____

_____

_____

_____

_____

_____

_____

_____

_____

I long to accomplish a great and noble task, but it is my chief duty to accomplish humble tasks as though they were great and noble. The world is moved along not only by the mighty shoves of its heroes, but also by the aggregate of the tiny pushes of each honest worker.

HELEN KELLER

MONEY AND FINANCES

An Introduction

> What will it profit a man if he gains the whole world, and loses his own soul?
>
> MARK 8:36 NKJV

what really counts

Every man in the world has invested himself in something. Some men spend their lives focusing on their financial investments—often with the worthy goals of providing for their families and building future security. While these goals are certainly admirable, the desire to obtain as much money as possible can become a lifelong obsession. Men who are consumed with the desire to increase their bank accounts are missing out on what matters most to the heart of God.

It's not hard to decipher how God feels about money; Jesus talks about it more than any other topic. Over and over again, He emphasizes the point that material wealth often goes hand in hand with spiritual poverty. Jesus says, "Yes, I tell you that it is easier for a camel to go through the eye of a needle than for a rich person to enter the kingdom of God" (Matthew 19:24 NCV). While there are plenty of wealthy people who serve God faithfully, he's talking about those who increase wealth selfishly and forfeit the eternal rewards gained from investing in the kingdom of God.

You've been given three things in your life to invest: your time, your talents, and your money. Are you investing yourself wisely in these three areas? It takes time to develop healthy, growing relationships with your wife and children, but nothing is more valuable. As you increase in a growing knowledge of God's Word, you'll know best how to be a good steward of the treasures he's given you.

> As surely as we receive blessings from Him, He will pour out blessings through us.
> OSWALD CHAMBERS

Money and Finances

What's Money Good For?

No one can serve two masters. The person will hate one master and love the other, or will follow one master and refuse to follow the other. You cannot serve both God and worldly riches.

MATTHEW 6:24 NCV

what really counts

The most successful marketers in the world know how to push your buttons to make you crave what they're selling. When you see a commercial for a car on TV, you're drawn to a lifestyle that whets your appetite. You see a happy man driving a big sports utility vehicle taking his family on an off-road adventure through the mountains, and it looks exciting. Or you see a red sports car careening around seaside curves, and you long for the freedom you're led to believe that car will bring.

But when advertisers entice you with the thrills of high living, they don't show you what you may have to sacrifice to get there. The short-lived goal of owning an expensive, new car may force you to slave extra hours away from home. Paul warns, "Immorality or any impurity or greed must not even be named among you, as is proper among saints" (Ephesians 5:3 NASB). God wants you to be free from the claws of greed and self-indulgence. Money that is earned and spent on temporary pleasures will not build up the kingdom of God.

It's not only your attitudes toward money that matter; the way you spend and invest your money also makes a lasting impression on your children as well. Do you see them content with their own possessions, or do they constantly whine and beg for more? There's no worse feeling than to watch a child tear through his birthday presents one after another without stopping to acknowledge the giver. James Dobson says, "It is my belief that excessive materialism in parents has the power to inflict enormous spiritual damage on our sons and daughters."

But if you have the attitude that money is your gift from God to be used wisely, you will feel free from the self-indulgent lifestyle that ensnares so many. Instead of snapping up whatever marketers dangle before you, ask yourself if you really need that item. What will owning it do to your financial freedom? There are many ways you can use your material blessings to enrich the lives of others. When you give a regular tithe, you show God that you have faith that He will use it to grow His kingdom. Ask God to give you a servant heart in the area of finances, and you'll find that your desire to please Him overcomes anything the advertisers toss your way. That's true freedom.

Money and Finances

What's Money Good For?

What Matters Most...

◎ Loving God more than your money.

◎ Trusting God that he'll provide for you and your family.

◎ Demonstrating self-control when it comes to those emotional urges to buy things you don't need.

◎ Maintaining a balance between the time and energy you spend at work as well as with your family.

◎ Communicating God's views on money to your family. Ultimately, they are watching you to see how you handle your resources.

What Doesn't Matter...

◎ Feeling like your life is in the slow lane because you've stepped off the corporate treadmill while you're raising your children at home.

◎ Giving up high-status symbols, such as new cars and exotic vacations that you can live without.

◎ Not being able to see into the future to make sure your family is provided for. That's where faith in God's Word must override your fears.

◎ Accumulating consumer clutter just because everybody else is. Marketers make you think you can't live without their irresistible stuff, but you can!

Focus Points...

Every good action and every perfect gift is from God. These good gifts come down from the Creator of the sun, moon, and stars, who does not change like their shifting shadows.
JAMES 1:17 NCV

Wealth gained by dishonesty will be diminished, but he who gathers by labor will increase.
PROVERBS 13:11 NKJV

People who long to be rich fall into temptation and are trapped by many foolish and harmful desires that plunge them into ruin and destruction.
1 TIMOTHY 6:9 NLT

Why do you spend money on what cannot nourish you and your wages on what does not satisfy you? Listen carefully to me: Eat what is good, and enjoy the best foods.
ISAIAH 55:2 GOD'S WORD

what really counts

I was once young and now I am old, but not once have I been witness to God's failure to supply my need when first I had given for the furtherance of His work.
WILLIAM CAREY

It is more blessed to give than to receive, but then it is also more blessed to be able to do without than to have to have.
SÖREN KIERKEGAARD

Money and Finances
It's All God's

> The earth belongs to the LORD, and every-
> thing in it—the world and all its people.
>
> PSALM 24:1 NCV

what really counts

There was once a rich and powerful man who had it all. He owned a vast, luxurious estate; thousands of head of cattle; and often held well attended, colorful feasts and parties. His home was filled with the laughter and love of his beautiful wife and ten children. On top of all this, he served God faithfully and was considered a blameless and upright man. He lacked absolutely nothing and was known as the greatest man among his people. Yet in an instant of sudden horror, he lost everything.

Of course, this is the story of Job. How would you have reacted if you found yourself in his position? Not only did he lose all of his children and wealth, Job was overcome by a nasty, painful disease. Instead of cursing God and running away to bask in self-pity, he held on to his faith and said, "Naked I came from my mother's womb, naked I'll return to the womb of the earth. GOD gives, GOD takes. God's name be ever blessed" (Job 1:21 MSG). There are not many who could have withstood such a test. In the end, God blessed the second half of Job's life more abundantly than the first, and he serves as an example to all generations after him.

Everything you have is a gift from God. Your home, your family, your financial portfolio—even your health—are all on loan from Him. You don't own anything; you're just a caretaker who is accountable to his master. Being a wise steward of your financial resources means that you will use your money to enrich the lives of others and build up God's kingdom. God expects you to use your money for His glory—not to waste it, but neither to neglect it. Can you say that you are holding onto your money loosely enough that your security rests in God alone?

Every Christian needs to give something back to God as a testimony to the Lord's ownership. Scripture says, "He who sows sparingly will also reap sparingly, and he who sows bountifully will also reap bountifully" (2 Corinthians 9:6 NKJV). When you're generous in helping others, it may not make sense in the eyes of your non-Christian family and friends. But Jesus says, "It is more blessed to give than to receive" (Acts 20:35 NCV). Through sharing, God's power over your finances is shown to be of utmost importance in your life.

Money and Finances
It's All God's

What Matters Most...

◎ Having a biblical view of money. Everything comes from God and belongs to Him, and your job is to be a wise steward.

◎ Giving back to God as a testimony to His ownership of your finances.

◎ Sowing abundantly so that you may also reap abundantly, according to Scripture.

◎ Thanking God for the gifts He has given to you, and praying

◎ Being willing to share with those in need.

What **Doesn't** Matter...

◎ Wanting to hold on to your possessions tightly. You don't really own them.

◎ Losing out against the Joneses, who manage to have it all (at least in your eyes).

◎ Comparing your lifestyle to your coworkers who put in more hours and move ahead, often at the expense of their personal lives.

◎ Doing without luxury items so you can give to God's kingdom.

◎ Wondering whether your giving is really making a difference in the world.

Focus Points...

Seek first the kingdom of God and His righteousness, and all these things shall be added to you.
MATTHEW 6:33 NKJV

Whoever loves money will never have enough money; whoever loves wealth will not be satisfied with it.
ECCLESIASTES 5:10 NCV

Whoever can be trusted with a little can also be trusted with a lot, and whoever is dishonest with a little is dishonest with a lot.
LUKE 16:10 NCV

Freely you have received, freely give.
MATTHEW 10:8 NKJV

what really counts

Lust for money brings trouble and nothing but trouble. Going down that path, some lose their footing in the faith completely and live to regret it bitterly ever after.
1 TIMOTHY 6:10 MSG

The first step in achieving financial freedom is to realize that since God is in complete control, all that we are, do, have, or ever will have must be transferred to Him.
LARRY BURKETT

The act of giving best reminds me of my place on earth. All of us live here by the goodness and grace of God.
PHILIP YANCEY

305

What Matters Most to Me About
Money and Finances

God is sovereign over your finances, and it is a test of your faith to be a wise steward. The way you invest and spend your mate-

◎ *God has given you three areas to invest in: your time, your talents, and your treasures. Would you say you are demonstrating a godly attitude in the management of these areas of your life.*

_____

_____

_____

_____

_____

_____

_____

_____

_____

◎ *Do you feel that you are being a wise steward of your financial resources? Why or why not?*

_____

_____

_____

_____

_____

_____

what really counts

◎ *Do you have a written list of financial goals for you and your family? Write down the five top goals here.*

_____

_____

_____

_____

_____

_____

_____

_____

_____

◎ *Ask God in a written prayer to show you how to be a good manager of the money he's given you. As the leader of your home, the way you handle your money will be passed along to your wife and children.*

_____

_____

_____

_____

_____

_____

_____

_____

_____

> Money as a form of power is so intimately related to the possessor that one cannot consistently give money without giving self.
>
> EDWARD W. BAUMAN

HEALTH

An Introduction

> God owns the whole works. So let people see God in and through your body.
>
> 1 CORINTHIANS 6:20 MSG

what really counts

The prophet Daniel was among a group of gifted and handsome young Hebrew men who were brought to serve at the court of the Babylonian King Nebuchadnezzar. Among the privileges of that exclusive group was the fact that they were fed the king's choicest food. But Daniel and his friends Shadrach, Meshach, and Abed-nego chose not to defile themselves with Nebuchadnezzar's delicacies. Instead they asked to eat only vegetables and water. Permission was granted on one condition: They had to stay at least as healthy as their peers.

Daniel understood that serving God meant serving God in his body. God honored that commitment by giving Daniel and his three friends health and strength that amazed the Babylonians. Daniel was just obeying the dietary laws set forth in Old Testament law. Those laws may seem overly complex and legalistic to modern-day Christians, but one thing comes through loud and clear in all those shalts and shalt-nots about eating and drinking: God cares what you do with your body.

You are free from the strict dietary laws of the Old Testament. But the spirit of the laws still stands: Your body is the temple of the Holy Spirit, and you should honor that temple through habits that build it up rather than breaking it down—by eating and drinking healthful things, by exercising regularly, by getting plenty of rest, by avoiding destructive habits. Real spirituality is about more than taking care of your spirit. It's about taking care of your body too.

> Joy and Temperance and Repose slam the door on the doctor's nose.
>
> HENRY WADSWORTH LONGFELLOW

Health
Serving God with Your Body

what really counts

If you ever fly, you've heard the spiel from the flight attendant: *In the event of a sudden loss of cabin pressure, oxygen masks will drop from the overhead area; if you have a small child with you, secure your own mask before assisting with theirs.* It seems a little selfish, making your child wait while you secure life-giving oxygen for yourself. But the logic is sound: An adult who has passed out for lack of oxygen can help neither his child nor himself. Sometimes the selfless thing to do is to take care of yourself.

If you want to take care of other people, you had better look after your own health. People depend on you. Your wife, your children, your parents, your coworkers, and many others need you to be strong on their behalf. If you're laid up in the hospital, there's a good chance you're receiving more than you're giving. There are times, of course, when sickness and physical suffering are unavoidable. Nobody's constitution is impervious to weakness. But you owe it to more people than yourself to take care of your health the best you can—to eat well, exercise, get plenty of exercise, and avoid habits that could wreck your body.

Your health is a gift. Like money or time or talents, it has been given to you in trust. You are the steward of your body just as you are the steward of those other things, and you aren't free to squander your health on junk food or cigarettes or a slothful lifestyle. Rather, you have a responsibility to use it to grow the kingdom of God. When you feel good and strong, when you have plenty of energy, you are better able to reach out to others and do the work God has called you to. When you're sick and tired and weak, your natural tendency is to turn your attention in toward self.

That's not to say that you can't serve God when you're in poor health. God has many reasons for taking away a person's good health, either temporarily or permanently. There is much to be learned in weakness and brokenness, not the least of which is how to reach out to others when you yourself are needy. But as far as it depends on you, it's important that you guard your health carefully. It's one of God's greatest gifts, and it's not to be taken for granted.

Health
Serving God with Your Body

What Matters Most...

◎ Honoring God with the one body He gave you.

◎ Your responsibility to those who love and depend on you. They need you to be as healthy as you can be.

◎ Only putting good things into your body.

◎ Praying that God will give you the motivation you need to take care of yourself.

◎ Thinking of the long-term implications of the choices you make today.

What **Doesn't** Matter...

◎ Laziness. Don't let that keep you from taking care of yourself; too many people depend on you.

◎ The idea that it's narcissistic to pay attention to your body. Sometimes taking care of yourself is the most selfless thing you can do.

◎ The inevitability of old age and death. Guard your health as long as you can.

◎ Wistful memories of a younger, healthier you. Do the best you can with what you have now.

◎ Feeling invincible to illness. You're not. Take care of yourself.

Focus Points...

Didn't you realize that your body is a sacred place, the place of the Holy Spirit? Don't you see that you can't live however you please, squandering what God paid such a high price for? The physical part of you is not some piece of property belonging to the spiritual part of you.
1 Corinthians 6:19 MSG

Dear friend, I pray that you may enjoy good health and that all may go well with you, even as your soul is getting along well.
3 John 2 NIV

Your light shall break forth like the morning, your healing shall spring forth speedily, and your righteousness shall go before you; the glory of the Lord shall be your rear guard.
Isaiah 58:8 NKJV

what
really
counts

It is the part of a Christian to take care of his own body for the very purpose that by its soundness and well-being he may be enabled to labor ... for the aid of those who are in want.

Martin Luther

The human body seems indestructible when we are young. However, it is incredibly fragile and must be cared for if it is to serve us for a lifetime.

James Dobson

Health
Choosing Wellness

You created my inmost being; you knit me together in my mother's womb. I praise you because I am fearfully and wonderfully made.

PSALM 139:13–14 NIV

In the movie *Chariots of Fire,* Olympic sprinter and missionary Eric Liddell speaks of the spiritual significance of his athletic ability. God made him fast, he says, "And when I run, I feel his pleasure." Have you ever experienced that? Have you ever felt God's pleasure in your physical being—in stretched limbs and a raised heart rate, in a perfect drop shot or a soaring jump shot? There's something spiritual about physical exertion, about making your body do what it was made to do. Quiet contemplation and prayer are vital to the life of faith, but Christianity isn't something that happens only in your heart and mind. Your whole self belongs to Christ, body and soul.

Your body is more than just a container for your soul. Your physical self is connected to your spiritual self in ways that no theologian or scientist or anybody else fully understands. You've experienced it—a spiritual malaise that turned out just to be a cold coming on, a spiritual high that gave you a renewed physical energy. If you're serious about tending to your spirit, you'd better be serious about tending to the body it inhabits.

It's worth noting that, according to the Bible, in heaven you will have a new glorified, perfect body. The lame will walk. The blind will see. Some eastern religions describe heaven as a place were disembodied spirits will dissolve into one great Over-spirit. But the Bible is clear that, just as on earth, in heaven your soul will have its residence in a body. That gives a hint as to the status of the physical body in the Christian tradition. The one you have now isn't perfect, but it's the only one you have for the time being, and the wise thing is to take care of it.

Your body is the temple of the Holy Spirit. It's a mind-blowing thing to think about. If the Holy Spirit lived in a building, wouldn't you want to make sure the roof didn't leak, the walls stayed painted and the cobwebs were swept away? In the same way, it's your responsibility to maintain your body. Keep a close eye on your spiritual heart, but have your physical heart checked out too. Eat good, healthful food even as you feast on God's Word. Rest in God's promises, and while you're at it, get plenty of rest for your body. Those are spiritual services too.

Health
Choosing Wellness

What Matters Most...

- ◎ The joy to be found in physical exertion. Feel God's pleasure.

- ◎ Recognizing that your body is the temple of the Holy Spirit. Maintain it.

- ◎ The unity of body and soul. You aren't just a soul being carried around in a body. Your body is you too.

- ◎ Rest. Even God rested after creating the universe.

- ◎ Gratitude. Health is a gift to be thankful for.

What **Doesn't** Matter...

- ◎ Being the fastest, the strongest, the most athletic. The important thing is staying healthy.

- ◎ Fad diets. They key is balance.

- ◎ Magazine images of ideal men. Exercise for health, not for vanity.

- ◎ The drive to over-exert. A healthy thing becomes unhealthy if you over-do it.

- ◎ Your busy schedule. Make time to exercise.

Focus Points...

Do not be fooled: You cannot cheat God. People harvest only what they plant.
GALATIANS 6:7 NCV

No discipline seems pleasant at the time, but painful. Later on, however, it produces a harvest of righteousness and peace for those who have been trained by it.
HEBREWS 12:11 NIV

A joyful heart is good medicine, but a broken spirit dries up the bones.
PROVERBS 17:22 NASB

Those who receive that rest which God promised will rest from their own work, just as God rested from his.
HEBREWS 4:10 GNT

what really counts

There is one who speaks like the piercings of a sword, but the tongue of the wise promotes health.
PROVERBS 12:18 NKJV

A man too busy to take care of his health is like a mechanic too busy to take care of his tools.
SPANISH PROVERB

When wealth is lost, nothing is lost; when health is lost, something is lost; when character is lost, all is lost.
BILLY GRAHAM

What Matters Most to Me About
Health

God gave you a body, mind, and soul. Being a complete man requires that you take care of each of those areas. If your body is falling apart, it can be hard to learn and grow spiritually.

◎ *When is the last time you had a check-up? Do you think you are in good shape?*

_____

_____

_____

_____

_____

what
really
counts

_____

_____

_____

◎ *Are there any areas where you feel you might need to be more careful, such as nutrition, exercise, weekend activities, or rest?*

_____

_____

_____

_____

_____

_____

_____

_____

_____

◎ *Write down three steps you want to take this week to start improving in those areas.*

_____

_____

_____

_____

_____

_____

_____

_____

_____

◎ *From those steps, develop a list of long-term goals you'd like to accomplish with your health. Share these goals with someone you care about, and ask them to hold you accountable!*

_____

_____

_____

_____

_____

_____

_____

_____

_____

> Our religious activities should be ordered in such a way as to have plenty of time for the cultivation of the fruits of solitude and silence.
>
> A. W. TOZER